Milo, Me an

The Begi

By Nicci Taylor

© Nicci Taylor 2018

This book is non-fiction. All the people and places are real. The events
took place in 2015

I dedicate this book to my Dad in heaven. My father instilled in me to always knock on a stranger's door as a stranger is just a friend you haven't met yet...

First and foremost, I must thank Milo, without whom this adventure could not have happened. I will be forever grateful to my family and close friends who were always there, holding a safety net, just in case. To Pip, my sister and constant support throughout. My mum, who still asks "when will this midlife crisis end?" And my son, Philip, who probably denies knowing me! Thank you to Jefferson Merrick, my editor, for making my book readable. Thank you to my friends, old and new, through social media, who followed my adventure and helped make it happen. And last of all I thank Me. Me, who had a dream. Me, who believed in my dream. And Me, who is still dreaming. Never give up on your dream...

Chapter 1

May 2015   The Plan

"Milo, I need you to pay attention to what I'm going to tell you."

He tilted his big, red, square head with each word I said, never taking his eyes off mine. Except for the occasional sly glance at my hands. Always check the hands, if they're closed chances are she could be holding a biscuit.

"We're going away. Me and you, we're going on an adventure."

He continued to stare at me, his big brown eyes questioning mine. I kept it short and to the point, after-all dogs recognise very few syllables.

I told him I loved him and he was the centre of my world, but I needed more. I need a man in my life. In fact, not just any man but my Mr Perfect man. So, the plan was I would leave the job I hated, I would sell absolutely everything I owned, buy a motor-home and go looking for Mr Perfect. Easy-peasy. Just like that. Job done. Happy ever after.

Milo had to be on-board with my plan, he just had to. He had the loudest bark I'd ever heard from a dog and this weapon would hopefully deter any potential murderers or the like on our adventure. But first and foremost, he was my best friend.

Milo had come into my life by default. My son, Philip, had pestered me for years to get a dog and I'd always stood my ground with a firm, No! But one evening, three years earlier, Philip said he needed to talk to me. He had to tell me something of the utmost importance. He hoped I'd understand how difficult a conversation this was for him but it needed to be said. Well at this point I was quite hysterical and begging for him to just tell me what was wrong.

"My girlfriend and I are going to have a baby." he said.

"A bbbaby, you're going to have a baby?" I spluttered.

"No, but I'm getting a dog." he exclaimed.

"Yes, yes of course, let's get a dog." I heard myself say.

And that's when Milo came into my life. The most handsome Fox Red Labrador I'd ever seen. Of course, Philip professed to the fact that he would walk him every day, pick up all the pooh and pay for everything. X-box interfered with that plan just about the same time my maternal instincts kicked in. Milo was mine. My Milo. Milo and me.

Our first year together was trying. Milo was a typical Labrador puppy. He ate everything. Nothing was safe from his tiny little pin teeth. If it fitted, it went in his mouth. Reading my mail was like doing jigsaw puzzles if Milo got to it first he shredded it and ate it. If even the tiniest thread appeared on a blanket he'd nibble away at it until he'd unravelled the lot. Stuffed animals had no chance of survival, even more so if they incorporated a squeak. Milo would ravish out their insides until the squeak was discovered. My house was scattered with dead, dismembered teddies. Dressing gown ties were a game of dangle and grab, as was any item of clothing possessing something he could latch his teeth into.

Milo loved laundry days. He would wag his tail furiously as I headed toward the washing machine and then dive into the basket to find a sock, always a sock. This in turn became a game of chase. He would charge through the whole house, bouncing off walls and furniture, sock in mouth beckoning for a game of tug of war. He always made me laugh. The more I laughed the more Milo would perform. He became like a child, a child who also figured out early on that if I'm talking on the telephone all he had to do was stick his nose in any out of bounds area and he would not be chastised but given a biscuit. Clever.

I, rather foolishly, kept biscuits in my pocket when he was a puppy. And now, even to this day, if anyone puts their hand in their pocket Milo will sit at their feet and wait patiently. He has even been known to poke his nose into stranger's pockets whilst waiting at pedestrian crossings and have a root around.

Milo...

Milo was so handsome, a fact declared by many a stranger. Although one day, as I proudly walked him down the road on his lead, a little boy of about seven spotted him. He pointed at Milo and exclaimed to his father, in a very strong Scouse accent:

"Arr ey, Dad look at the ginger dog!"

"He's not ginger, he's Fox Red." I corrected him, in my poshest accent "Fox Red!"

Milo was my best friend. My constant companion. I couldn't envisage ever doing anything without him.

Milo was still staring at me, rather vacantly now, but the little bump on top of his head had protruded. The bump that tells me he loves me. His happy bump. So, I gave him the biscuit, patted his head and sat down to try and decide how to have this same conversation with my family.

"Oh, don't be ridiculous!" exclaimed my mum.

"How are you going to afford it? You can't just sell everything, what will you do when you get back?"

Back? I thought. I hadn't planned on the back bit. Why would I want to come back when my intention is to go forward. Happy ever afters don't involve going back to the unhappy bit. She didn't understand but luckily my sister Pip did.

"Oh wow, do it Nicci, what have you got to lose?" Pip encouraged.

"You hate your job, it's making you ill and so unhappy. Yes, it's a madcap idea but I can't think of anybody else who could make this happen." she enthused.

"Oh Pip, I can do this can't I? I shouldn't just sit here and wait for my life to happen. I should get out there and make it happen." I replied.

I knew Pip would be on board. Ever since her brain haemorrhage fifteen years ago I'd been there for Pip. My world was her world, my thoughts were hers. But now she'd met the man of her dreams, she had her own little world and she didn't need to live in mine. She was happy and that's what she wanted for me. Pip would back me all the way.

Now Philip's reaction was the one I dreaded the most. My boy, my handsome, intelligent and ever so confident boy. It had always been just me and him, no father on the scene, just the two of us. That is until girlfriends came into the mix. It had taken me many years, and many girlfriends, to realise I was not the centre of his world. He didn't need me now, he was doing exceptionally well without me. But this made me happy, this told me I'd done an all right job. He was focused and knew what he wanted in life. I just hoped he'd understand what I wanted.

"Whatever makes you happy, Mum." he mumbled.

That was probably the best I was going to get at this point. His thoughts were probably more on what he'd be roped in to help with. Due to no one else's fault but my own Philip was a rather lazy young man. Although I did always admire his charm at being able to persuade other people to do things for him.

Now I had Pip backing me all the way, Philip's blessing and my mum who thought I'd totally lost my mind. But most importantly I believed in myself. For the first time ever, I felt like I could take control and direct my life. It was such a wonderful feeling. I felt rather grown-up.

Grown Up and at the controls. That's how I felt. It had only taken me nearly fifty years but here I was, me making the decision on how my life would be from now on. I could go anywhere I wanted to go, meet anyone I chose to meet, I would do whatever my mind decided. I would not be controlled by a job, a destination, a person or a situation. I would explore every given day and be grateful for the next. My life would become my adventure.

Of course, I'd made decisions before but they were decisions for survival, not adventure. I'd ended relationships, I'd changed jobs, I'd moved house, but never because I just wanted to.

Now I was doing something just for me. I was about to walk through life like Milo 'I was about to wander off the path'. I would create my adventure and hopefully meet the man of my dreams on the journey.

Here is an extract from my blog, written at the time.

The plan – 25th May

Well I've decided...Milo and Me are going to live in a camper van! This is very early on in the process and I don't actually own a camper van or in fact have ever been inside one, but this is what we have planned. I informed Milo this morning of my plan and I swear he looked impressed...that little lump appeared on top of his head, the one that tells me he loves me and is happy.

So, the plan.   As my work contract ends on the last day of May and I will be paid until July I have a little time on my side to prepare. Argh! Where do I start? Downsizing a three-bed house with sixteen years-worth of stuff into a small metal box on wheels, that's a hell of a lot of car boot sales. But like I said it's just stuff. When I first left home I had one suitcase and rented a box room with two crazy men in Chester. Surely, I don't need all this stuff I have acquired along the way? I need to act as if I'm going on a long holiday, pack essentials and just let go of excess baggage. Excess baggage... Beds, sofas, cooker, teddies, photos, a large collection of shoes and handbags, kitchen draws overflowing with might need that one-day items, pots, pans and I haven't even got to the garden shed yet. July now seems far too close.

Happy birthday to me - 26th May

49 today...So 12 months until the big 50, 12 months to have an adventure in my 40's, 12 months until I become a spinster at 50! Been awake since 7am, don't think Milo remembered it was my birthday so no lie in today. There is a decent tide so am thinking beach walk this morning, then home to do some more decluttering and birthday meal tonight.

Après birthday - 27th May

Well I received the grand total of 3 birthday cards... mother, sister and daughter and Milo ate the mother card! But on a happier note I had 48 birthday messages on Facebook, does that mean if Facebook was never invented I would have received 51 birthday cards?! I'm going to kid myself that is true ;)

I had a meal with my three birthday card givers last night which was quite pleasant until my mother made it quite clear that she isn't very impressed with my Milo and Me adventure :(I am sure it is just a natural mother concern and she is thinking worst case scenario. I just need to convince her all will be fine.

Chapter 2

Me. Miss Nicci Taylor. Nicci in the middle, the title and the surname either side had never changed. Jobless, boyfriend-less, about to be homeless and fast approaching or even slightly past my mid-life. This is not how I had my life planned out. When I was growing up I actually believed I would marry a prince, Prince Andrew to be precise. He was the slightly better looking one of the three. It didn't happen.

But I did continue to believe I would at some point be a wife to someone. I'd had a few long-term relationships but none had resulted in marriage. I always felt there was something missing in these relationships, I never felt complete. Each relationship had me believe he was not my Mr Right.

I did receive a few marriage proposals, even one by text. But for some reason I always chose to hold out for a better offer. Alas it never came.

And so here I am, a spinster approaching fifty. Spinster, that is what they write on your death certificate if you die single. I will not let this happen, which is why I decided to get off my backside and go out there and find my Prince Charming.

I'd already tried most of the usual routes available to meet men, including numerous dating sites, with some hilarious outcomes. The longest on-line courtship lasted a few weeks, the shortest about an hour.

The gentleman lasting a few weeks was mainly through default as he worked away in Afghanistan and was rarely in the UK. We'd had two dates in Liverpool when he invited me to fly out to his second home in Cyprus. I hummed and arhed with this invitation. Echoes of my mother's voice "he could murder you out there." were rationalised with "he had opportunity to murder me in Liverpool."

So off I flew to Cyprus for what I hoped would be a romantic getaway. It was not to be. My first clue to this was on the journey to the airport. He sat in the front seat of the taxi leaving me alone in the back. Even on the airplane I sat in the window seat and he chose to leave the middle seat between us empty and sat in the aisle seat. Every morning, for breakfast, he made disgusting green liquid protein drinks for us and then he went off on twenty-mile runs. He then seemed happy to spend the rest of the day lying on the opposite settee to me, watching old black and white movies on the TV. I spent most days lying alone by the pool eyeing up the part-time gardener. After a few days I decided to question him.

"Do you find me attractive, Marty?" I asked.

"Yes Nicci, why?"

"Well you've hardly come near me all week." I said, my bottom lip pouting out. "I kind of thought, what with me wandering around in a bikini all day, you'd be unable to keep your hands off me. I thought we'd be at it like rabbits. I had visions of you grabbing me from behind, whilst I was washing the dishes, and indulging me in hours of passion..." I exclaimed.

Marty stared at me, rather blankly, and then replied

"I haven't seen you wash the dishes, Nicci."

He spent the rest of the week watching TV. I spent my time by the pool lusting after the gardener. I never saw Marty again.

My on-line date that lasted an hour was quite odd too. I'd telephoned a girlfriend to tell her I was meeting him that evening. She was in the same line of business as him and asked of his details. I couldn't remember all the details so whilst chatting to her I Googled his business name. And there in front of me on the first page of Google was his photograph under the headline 'Local Man Charged with Rape'.

"You can't go on a date with a rapist!" exclaimed my friend.

"No, hang on a minute," I said "there's more info here."

As I scrolled down I could see further write-ups. A photograph of him on the court steps, headlined 'Not Guilty'.

"You still can't go and meet this guy." my friend protested.

But the more I read about his story the more I felt I had to go and meet him. My friend had said there's no smoke without fire but I thought to myself what if it had been my own son, falsely accused of rape? What if any future potential girlfriend refused to even meet him because he'd been accused of something he didn't do. So, I went on the date. My friend actually offered to sit discreetly at another table in the pub in case I needed her help. I assured her I only intended to have one drink and then leave to go home alone.

Before I'd even arrived at the pub my date had texted to say he had arrived and was waiting. When I got there, he had ordered a drink for me, on the assumption that I liked white wine. His demeanour was relaxed. He sat quite far back in his chair, one foot crudely resting on his knee, both elbows resting on the arms of the chair, a Marlboro Light in one hand, a large wine glass in the other. His shirt cuffs were undone and floating around his wrists. I also noticed his shoes were high-heeled. His conversation was confident bordering on arrogant. He was excessively complimentary of my appearance.

I stayed for an hour. I'd informed him, before I arrived, that I could only stay for an hour as I was attending a family party later in the evening. As I was driving away he texted me to say he'd enjoyed my company. When I arrived at my sister's he texted again to say it would be great to arrange another date. This was immediately followed by asking when we could meet again. Ten minutes later he texted me to ask why I hadn't replied to his texts. I quickly replied saying I was with family and would try and message him later. Ten minutes later he texted me asking what I liked for breakfast. This pattern of events went on late into the night until I finally sent a message explaining I wouldn't be up for a second date but wished him every success in finding the right girl for him. His reply was a stream of obscenities stating that he didn't like me anyway and the phrase 'you're far too old a hag for me'. I was about three years older than him. Small man syndrome was the phrase bobbing about in my head and my friend's words: 'there's no smoke without fire'.

Over the years I'd even tried entering various TV shows that profess to find you love, but I never even got to the selection stages. I did many an evening supermarket shopping trip scouting for eligible men on their way home from the office, scanning trolleys for evidence of them being single, i.e. no nappies, lady's toiletries or meals for two. I endured evenings stood in bars, for hours on end, being chatted up by mainly drunks looking for a one-night stand.

I even explored some rather ridiculous ideas including putting myself up for sale on e-Bay. I positioned myself in the antiques and collectables section assuming I may be found by an Arabian prince who would whisk me away to an exotic land and fall madly in love with me. No, that didn't happen. I sold for £2.60 to a weirdo from Nottingham who sent some equally weird messages. I had to withdraw the sale citing damaged goods.

Another, more recent, crazy plan involved placing Milo in the pet re-homing section on both Gumtree and Pets4Homes. The advert included me and him as a package. I listed his needs as food and bed. My needs list was slightly longer: my own bedroom, large kitchen, bath, central heating, Wi-Fi connection, garden area, etc. Pets4homes removed my advert pretty much straight away but Gumtree ran it for a few weeks. I actually received some reasonable offers including sharing a barge on a canal with a nomad type gentleman, pitching up a tent in an elderly man's back garden, and a house share with a gentleman if he could manage to convince his wife of the idea.

Thinking back, I'd spent most of my life coming up with crazy ideas. Even as a ten-year-old child I'd written to the makers of Smarties sweets asking if I could appear in their next TV advert and receive free Smarties for life.

No doubt my daftest idea was back in the nineties when I was working as an Air Hostess in Edinburgh for Air UK.

It was around 1990 and Aunty Gwen had come to stay for the weekend. A very large lady with an equally large personality. We all sat round the kitchen table with a pot of tea and custard cream biscuits, eaten mainly by Aunty Gwen. She then proceeded to tell us about her daughter who was now living in London City. Oh, she was living a wonderful lifestyle and had got herself a job as an 'escort'. This involved going to the likes of opera, theatre, ballet and fine dining restaurants with well-to-do gentlemen. She was paid large amounts of money and apparently gave nothing in return other than her company.

Well this all sounded rather interesting to me and my sister Pip. We were currently working as cabin crew out of Edinburgh airport. We both operated short haul routes that afforded us a lot of time off and we had been contemplating supplementing our income. So that evening we sat down and decided we too could do what Aunty Gwen's daughter was doing. Days off spent at the theatre, eating fine food with interesting gentlemen, and the bonus of being paid for it! We reached for the Yellow Pages and as luck would have it the first page produced 'Angels Escort Services'. We rang immediately to request an interview. Surprisingly they answered the phone even though it was rather late in the evening... After a few initial enquiries we had achieved ourselves an interview for the very next day with a lady named Marcia, no surname provided.

The rest of our evening was spent updating our CVs and deciding what to wear. I settled on a smart grey trouser suit with a satin striped shirt, including rather fashionable shoulder pads. Pip went for tailored black trousers matched with her very expensive tartan blazer.

The next morning as we were unsure of directions we decided to drive to Ingleston railway station and park the car there, where we would then take a taxi to said address. On arrival we approached the rank of black cabs and asked the first driver if he could take us to our address. He gave us a rather bemused look and said, "Hop in, ladies."

After a short journey he pulled up outside a row of rather run-down terraced houses. We questioned him on our whereabouts and he just smiled and pointed to the end terrace. There was no sign or advertisement on the door so we just knocked and waited. After what seemed ages the door opened a few inches and a rather large German Shepherd dog poked his head out and snarled. Behind him was Marcia, a large bosomed woman wearing very little and adorned with crude tattoos. We introduced ourselves and confirmed our appointment. Marcia took us into a little room towards the back of the house and told us to take a seat.

This room reminded me of a staff room in a back-street garage. The walls were adorned with posters of naked girls. The telephone had what looked like oil stained finger marks all over the hand piece. The armchairs were of tatty, ripped and stained fabric. We both cautiously sat down, CV's on laps. The German Shepherd decided to sit right in front of me with his head on my knee, slobbering on my CV.

Marcia then questioned us on why we had applied for this position. We both enthused about how much free time we had available, how we both loved theatre and the likes and what sociable escorts we thought we would make. Part way through this conversation a young girl burst into the room, wearing only a pair of panties and grabbed a bottle of baby oil from the table. Marcia then asked if we had any questions. I decided to bite the bullet and enquired how much money we could potentially earn? Marcia leant back in her chair, stroked her rather hairy chin, and said "it depends how far you're willing to go" to which I replied "Oh I have my own car so I'm quite happy to travel as far as Inverness on occasion."

Marcia never got back to us. Prostitution was to be one of the rare job opportunities at which I did not succeed...

I worked as cabin crew for about ten years. During an era when we were called Air Hostesses. Our uniform was pristine, we wore hats and gloves, a summer and winter mix. A one-hour flight usually consisted of complimentary drinks trolley, hot meal with complimentary wine, tea and coffee, complimentary liqueur trolley, second teas and coffee and finished off with hot towels. We even handed out boiled sweets for take-off and landing. Nowadays you're lucky to get a free seat belt on-board.

When people asked what you did for a living your reply was always received with remarks like "oh wow, I always wanted to do that." or "how glamorous." "bet you have loads of dishy pilot boyfriends."

Problem was, that is what I thought before I became an Air Hostess. I did always want to be one, I did think it would be glamorous and I did think I would fall in love with a dashing young pilot. Truth is, it was blooming hard work and the majority of pilots were not dashing or young. I think it also hindered my boyfriend prospects as I was often told 'I always used to fancy you but being an Air Hostess I thought you wouldn't look twice at me'. I rarely got chatted up. Except on one flight...

I was flying back to Edinburgh and a gentleman passenger towards the back of the aircraft had caught my eye. He was rather good looking and I was aware he was checking me out. When I reached his row with the drinks trolley I slammed the brakes on so hard I think I nearly broke the knee caps of my colleague. I leant over to my handsome passenger and asked him what he would like to drink from the bar whilst giving him my biggest smile. We struck up some flirty chit chat before I had to move down the cabin.

When we landed in Edinburgh my handsome passenger asked me for my telephone number and without a second thought I ripped off a headrest cover and wrote it down for him.

Trouble was, back then we had no such thing as mobile phones and therefore I ensued a few days of constantly picking up the house phone to check it was definitely working. And then he called. He sounded just as sexy as I remembered. He told me he was planning a night out on the town in Edinburgh that evening. He explained he was a successful property developer and had just secured a lucrative contract in the city. He was taking his whole work force out to celebrate and would love me to join them. How could I refuse I thought? And it wasn't difficult to persuade Pip to come along too.

My main problem was I was meant to be operating a flight that evening. So, slightly guiltily, I phoned in sick. I told myself it was worth it.

The evening was raucous. Pip and I were treated like princesses. My handsome passenger introduced us to his whole team, Joe the plumber, Ricky the joiner, Jack the brickie, etc. We had such a fun night. I had the undivided attention from my beau and so when he asked me back to his I thought why not? This could be the beginning of a beautiful romance. Pip was quite happy to stay in the company of his workforce so off we went.

Early the next morning Pip was knocking at his front door. We let her in and made a pot of coffee. We sat round the kitchen table discussing what a fun night we'd all had. I asked Pip if she'd been treated well by his team of employees.

"Oh yes," she replied "I was provided with a lovely comfy couch, no funny business and given money for a taxi to collect you, Nicci."

"Aw that's nice," I said "They seem to like their boss."

"Yes, they do." Pip said, giving my beau a sly glance "They like their manager very much, their Dundee Football Club manager, that's a decent 'team' you have there."

Not much more came of my romance. Other than I was hauled into the office at work amidst rumours of me not officially being sick that night and accusations of me dating a passenger. Of course, I denied it all and still feel bad about that today. Well, a little bit.

On reflection I'd always been rather unlucky in love. And evidently it wasn't for the want of trying.

Single no more, I decided. I had determination and a vivid enough imagination to take the bull by the horns and give it one last try before reaching the big five 'O'. I will be a bride. I will be a wife. I will find my Mr Perfect.

Chapter 3

So that's how my adventure began.

I began my preparation by creating a keep box. I found a large solid container and began to fill it with my most precious items. This included my, oh so very private, diary of over twenty-five years, which in turn gave me the notion to 'blog' my adventure. I began writing the adventure of 'Milo and Me'...

So, the plan was set in place. Now I just needed to put it into action. All I had to do was sell absolutely everything I owned, raise as much money as possible, buy a motor-home and drive off into the wilderness. The wilderness didn't scare me. I didn't care where in the world I lived because I'd spent my whole life with a feeling of not belonging. I'd felt like a visitor wherever I was, so moving around in a motor-home would suit me fine. My family had moved house so many times I'd lost count, I'd been the new girl in so many schools and invariably struggled to fit in. I'd had so many different jobs it had proved difficult to keep up friendships. So maybe I did belong, belong in the wilderness. Okay, so the plan wasn't quite the wilderness, I had in mind Scotland. I'd lived there at one point in my life and felt there was much more of it left to explore. And I did think the Scottish accent was attractive in a man. Scotland it was then, first step, let the adventure begin.

The hardest part of any given task is the beginning. Be it the ironing pile or adjusting your whole life. I could daydream to my heart's content about how my adventure would transpire, but putting it into action was all too real. Where do I start? I despaired. With a list I decided. Big lists, little lists, sub-lists, little sub-lists, an absolute list full of lists. But it was a start and if I could get just one tick on my list it would be my beginning.

Car boot sales are not much fun at the best of times. Why on earth they have to begin so early in the morning has always mystified me. But, if I was going to sell the entire contents of a three-bed semi, then car boots it was. Unfortunately, my car was a small KA so filling the boot was going to have to be a regular occurrence. I started off small, as in gathering anything I didn't use on a daily basis, that way it felt like just a normal clear out of 'stuff'. Then I made myself a rule that if it didn't belong in my motor-home it didn't belong in my life, trouble was as I didn't yet have a motor-home I had no idea what I should be keeping. I obviously knew my three-piece suite and the like wouldn't fit but 'stuff' like pots, pans, cushions, bedding, pictures, oh my, the list was endless. That's when my piles came into action, and no not the painful strain. I had piles to sell, piles to keep, piles to maybe keep, piles to give to friends or family and piles to bin. Overnight my house became an array of piles, really quite overwhelming.

It's amazing what items you find in your own home that you didn't even know you had. Hidden under the stairs, deep in the bottom of wardrobes, inside old suitcases or even in the pocket of a forgotten old coat. Items I found included; unused crochet sets, broken curling tongs, three drinking flasks, and a staggering amount of odd Tupperware boxes, to name but a few. My best find was a ten-pound note inside an old handbag. I also found two snooker cues behind the wardrobe in the spare bedroom. But Philip insisted that he 'needed' them. He had never asked of their whereabouts since they had been stuffed behind that wardrobe, for over four years!

My day to day life now consisted of an early morning walk for Milo, meet Pip for coffee, bone for Milo, then back to the house to sort 'stuff'. I spent hours sorting through a lifetime of memories, reminiscing over old love letters, laughing at dated photos, crying into kept baby clothes.

I was constantly on-line selling my larger household items for the best possible prices. Desperately trying to raise as much money as possible to make this dream a reality. If nothing else I was determined I was to have my happy ever after, my true love, my dream wedding, my harmonious blissful life.

But sadly, the pot of money wasn't getting much bigger. In fact, it was positively paltry. My car boots were raising on average no more than fifty pounds a time. And listening to folk barter you down to a measly ten pence, for a dress that provided some of my best nights out, was depressing.

My fund had to increase and had to increase quick.

So, I came up with a plan. I decided I would ask for help. Help in the form of begging but that's how desperate I was. I'd read stories of people who had set up funds for help in their life, be it a lifesaving operation or paying off their gas bill. I roped Pip in on this idea and persuaded her it was to be her idea. She was to write a piece on how my dream needed to come true and set up a fund to help make it happen. Millionaires far and near would plough money into my fund overnight, maybe even that Arabian Prince would just whisk me away and fulfil my dream instantly. But no. It didn't quite happen like that. I gave Pip, my mum and my son all the money from my pot and they pretended to kick start the donations, with kind words of encouragement. Three other friends kindly made donations and one anonymous person. So, in fact all I had was my own money, less the commission charge, and a small amount of hard earned cash from my dear friends. Put together with all the heart-breaking stories I read of other funds I felt pretty awful. This plan was not going to work. Life's not like that.

But life's a funny old game. I didn't quite know how the media worked but it crept into my life that day and bit me on the bum.

A journalist from The Sunday Post read of my fund and got in contact with me. The Sunday Post is a weekly newspaper published in Dundee, Scotland. It is mainly a mix of news, human interest stories and short features. He thought my planned adventure was a marvellous idea and asked if he could write a small article about Milo and Me heading up to Scotland, for his newspaper.

That small article turned into a two-page spread which then got picked up by media outlets I'd never even heard of. The story of Milo and Me went around the world, I kid you not. I ended up doing many interviews on various radio shows, was approached by numerous TV companies and hounded by magazine publications. Googling my name was a bizarre and worldwide experience. I was so often headlined as 'ex air hostess' or 'single mum' and written about on-line in so many foreign languages that it was only my photograph that told me it was me.

One of my radio interviews was with the lovely Kaye Adams for BBC Radio Scotland and in all honesty, it was just like chatting to a friend on the telephone.   Most of my radio interviews were enjoyable, I never really imagined anybody was listening, it was just me and the interviewer having a conversation. I was just sad that Milo was unable to join in.

Extract from one newspaper...

Home | News | U.S. | Sport | TV&Showbiz | Australia | Femail | Health | Science | Money

Latest Headlines | Femail | Fashion Finder | Food | Beauty | Gardening | Blogs | Baby Blog | Discounts

'My perfect man hasn't turned up, so I'm going to find him': Air hostess sells all of her possessions to buy camper van and will travel around Scotland looking for love

- Nicci Taylor, 49, from the Wirral, Merseyside, is looking for her dream man
- She is selling all of her possessions apart from some clothes and her dog
- Nicci bought a camper van and hopes to find love while touring Scotland

By CAROLINE MCGUIRE FOR MAILONLINE
PUBLISHED: 14:26, 7 June 2015 | UPDATED: 16:47, 7 June 2015

       1.9k shares ♥**288** View comments

A woman is selling everything she owns, buying a camper van and heading to Scotland - to search for the man of her dreams.

Nicci Taylor hopes to find love as she travels through the Highlands after a life devoted to looking after others.

The 49-year -old mother, who fell in love with Scotland when she worked in Edinburgh as an air hostess, says she has decided the time is right to put herself first for once.

From all this publicity I got so many messages of support through social media and my blog figures shot up. I remember saying to Pip, when I first published my blog, that three people had read it. I was so excited that three people whom I had never met were reading my blog, now there were thousands. My 'friends' list grew tenfold and I had some rather interesting proposals from men near and far, ranging from marriage proposals to meeting me in a lay-by for a night of passion.

I read each and every one of these messages and tried my utmost to reply to them all, obviously declining the lay-by offer.

From these messages I struck up conversations with a select few and built up some virtual friendships which I have to this day. I was pleasantly surprised to have received quite a few decent invitations from gentlemen living in Scotland, asking me to visit them when on my travels with Milo. They all seemed to own dogs, maybe that drew me in?

So, I made a list of four 'potential' gentlemen I would definitely go and visit on my quest. Hoping one of them might provide my happy ever after.

I also came up with another plan. A not so crazy plan this time. I was now quite aware I had a small army of gentlemen following my adventure through social media and I did feel rather privileged with this attention. I felt I should channel this attention in a positive way. So, I made the decision that on my journey I would promote awareness into a cause close to my heart. Prostate Cancer. The one that stole my Daddy. Sadly, my father died of this cruel cancer as his symptoms were not picked up early enough. My father was one of life's gentlemen. The life and soul of the party. And boy did he live life to the full. He was and still is an inspiration to me and I knew for a fact that if he were still alive he would be trying to join me on this adventure. I contacted some local charities and was able to gather enough information to hopefully spread some awareness of this horrible disease. On my journey if I was able to educate even just one man to recognise the early warning signs of Prostate Cancer then someone, somewhere could keep their Daddy a little longer than I could.

Chapter 4

Praise the Lord! My employment contract had ended, and I was now officially unemployed. I felt so happy. It's hard to explain how much I hated that job. Having spent ten years working as a receptionist, in a local health spa, I had chosen to broaden my horizons, and increase my meagre salary, by applying for a top-notch banking job I'd seen advertised locally. I beefed up my CV by using a bit of copy and paste from my son's CV and applied for this highly paid position on a whim. Somehow, I got the job.

I then spent the next twelve months in complete stress mode. My position entailed the refunding of PPI to bank customers, through a complex and baffling process. The pressure to follow the process, which constantly changed, was exhausting. I cried nearly every day, as did most employees. I even ended up on antidepressants from my doctor. It was quite possibly the worst job I'd ever had. But, I was paid a ridiculous amount of money without which I could never had made my adventure happen. Sometimes bad things happen for a good reason, I told myself.

Around this time my mum seemed to be coming round to the idea. If nothing else she could see how determined I was and that I was actually going to go through with this adventure. Pip was, as ever, my constant support and Philip even let me sell some of his stuff. One day when I returned home I found a small pile of items on my dining room table, from Philip, consisting of two pairs of leather shoes and four smart shirts. How kind I thought and I duly added them to my pile in the boot of the car and went upstairs to run one of my luxurious baths. Baths were one of the things I knew I was going to miss the most. I've always been a bath girl so lately I'd been having two a day. Whilst I was soaking in the bath I received a text from Philip.

'Hi, Mum, can you iron those shirts and polish my shoes by tomorrow?'

'Ha-ha very funny' I replied

'??' Philip texted back

That's when I realised he wasn't actually joking, he truly had brought them round to my house to be ironed and polished. Some sons just never stop needing their mum. Items were immediately removed from the car boot and obviously prepared for son's visit. I had to make the most of my remaining mum duties.

My house was now beginning to look a bit sparse. Faded squares on walls where pictures had once hung. Mantelpieces minus ornaments. Duvet covers hanging over my bedroom window having sold my curtains. An echo feeling all around as more and more furniture was sold. I had a mixture of feelings at this point. I flitted between 'oh my God what have I done?' to 'Wow, I feel so cleansed'.

My mum was so on board now, she called me one afternoon regarding a motor-home she'd seen locally for sale. So Pip, Mum and I trotted off to view it. Gross is an understatement. Personally if I was selling anything I'd spruce it up before a viewing. But no, this motor-home looked like someone had died in it. Now I'm not scared of a bit of cleaning but this motor-home needed binning. There was rotten mouldy food crusted onto the oven, dirty scummy rims around the sink, remnants of something looking like vomit in the toilet and the fabric interior was so tatty and moth eaten it was beyond repair. My heart sank. Even this motor-home was way above my budget. How was I ever going to afford one that didn't have me living like a tramp.

My mum and Pip made the usual 'don't worry, something will turn up' noises. But I headed home with a weary feeling.

At home I poured myself a large glass of wine and curled up on the couch with Milo.

"What have I done Milo?" I cried into my glass.

Not only had I activated this crazy plan but I'd told the whole world about it. People were contacting me on a daily basis telling me how inspiring I was. Imploring me with sad stories of how they would love to do what I am doing but alas they are held back with illness, children, careers, fear and the like. But, how encouraging to read about me, and wishing me every success and happiness.

I poured another large glass and cuddled into Milo.

"Milo if I don't make this happen not only am I letting myself down I'm letting down a whole lot of random strangers." He stared at me with his big, sad, Labrador eyes and let out a little whimper, he understood. Oh, the pressure was on me now.

I decided to trail round some motor-home sale sites just in the hope they might have an old, neglected and extremely cheap motor-home hidden away at the back. The one they couldn't display on their forecourt. The one nobody wanted to view let alone purchase. But it seemed cheap started at over twenty thousand, well above my budget. I did get chatting to a rather friendly salesman and told him of my planned adventure. He said he couldn't believe I was single and took my phone number promising to call if a suitable motor-home came into his possession. And message me he did, that very evening. He basically propositioned me with the offer of a loan of a motor-home in return that I provide him with services of a sexual nature. I must admit I considered this proposition, for about three seconds, then politely declined.

Whilst trailing around garages I came across a local garage advertising to buy second hand cars. I decided to pop in for a price on my KA. I was greeted by a lovely couple, Paul and Roz, who took a great interest in my planned adventure. They also offered me, what I thought, was an excellent cash price for my car. They were so friendly and even offered to help me find a suitable Motor-home through their contacts. My faith in human nature was once again restored.

Gumtree. My new best friend. I'd already sold various pieces of furniture through Gumtree and now I'd seen a Motor-home for sale not too far away in Manchester. The pictures looked decent, didn't look too grubby. The price was reasonable for the age of it. The specs meant nothing to me, height, weight, engine size etc. My interest was the interior in which I'd live. Ignorance is bliss in my world.

So once again Pip, Mum and I trotted off, this time to Manchester, to view this Motor-home.

We found the address, eventually. It was a large housing estate full of huge speed bumps. Speed bumps were, I was to discover, to become the bane of my life.

We were greeted by a jovial man sporting a tight fitting vest, football shorts and adorned with various tattoos. He was very chatty and seemed to know everyone who walked by the house, most being relatives, and we were introduced to all of them.

Eventually, jangling a large bunch of keys, he opened the door of the motor-home parked on his drive and let us in.

I got a warm and happy feeling straight away. This felt good. I was already doing that house hunting thing of placing my belongings into each room. OK, so I didn't have rooms as such and I certainly wasn't filling it with furniture. But I could already see where I'd blue tack my favourite photos and which colour cushions I'd scatter on the couches.

Basically the floor plan was: driver and passenger seat; two side benches running behind them, padded and housing underneath storage; a large cabin bed above the driver seat accessed by a ladder; a compact bathroom at the rear of the vehicle housing a toilet and a sink. The kitchen, consisting of cooker, hob, sink and fridge ran along the rear of van adjacent to the back door, or would that be the front door?

It was perfect, a home from home, albeit smaller.

The jovial man was busily trying to explain electrics and pumps to me and flicking an array of switches to demonstrate. I was still at this point blissfully choosing curtain fabric in my head.

He explained to me he was having an MOT this week and all being well it was mine.

Happy was an understatement.

I'd already decided this tired, extremely old, slightly rusty and not the most attractive Motor-home was to be my home. Home for Milo and me. My house on wheels to carry me on my adventure. My chariot to my happy ever after. My magic carpet to fly me to my prince. But not until I'd made those curtains.

Milo and Me in The Beast...

Chapter 5

The MOT was a success, my final wage was in my bank and I was heading to Manchester to purchase my Motor-home. Pip's boyfriend was to sit with me on the journey back home. I'd never driven anything much bigger than a saloon car at this point so was, needless to say, a little nervous.

A choke, no power steering, no electric windows, handbrake on my right, ignition key on left side of steering wheel and turn towards me to start, a mass of height above me and a rear view mirror which gave me a stunning view of my kitchen. Never mind the width and length of this vehicle, I'd never felt so scared driving such a beast. And that's when I named him. The Beast. My Beast. What a Beast.

And we all got back in one piece.

I couldn't wait to pimp The Beast. Within hours of our return I had on the rubber gloves and a bucket of bleach to hand. Pip's boyfriend gave me a quick lesson on how to plug into the mains electric and the kettle was subsequently switched on. Next I introduced Milo to his new home. I was so worried he may not be comfortable with this, which would definitely throw a spanner into the works. Erring on the edge of caution I placed some of his favourite biscuits in the kitchen cupboard and made a big fuss of retrieving them for him once inside.

Result! He didn't want to leave the van.

As I was bobbing in and out the van, carrying bits and pieces from my house, a lady approached me.

"Is this your motor-home?" she enquired.

I thought she was going to complain of my off-street parking and sheepishly replied "yes"

"Oh, how lovely! Are you off on your holidays?"

I told her of my forthcoming adventure, which was certainly not a holiday, but how excited I was. She told me all about her travels to Scotland many years ago and recommended some of her favourite haunts. We stood for ages having a lovely chat, which was quite funny really, because she lived next-door-but-one to me and had done for the past sixteen years, yet we'd never exchanged more than a 'hello' prior to this.

She said goodbye and told me if there was anything she could do to help all I had to do was knock. How lovely, I thought.

The next week or so was a whirlwind of curtain making, picture hanging, cushion scattering and generally covering anything I could find with fur fabric and fairy lights. I did have to hold back slightly as my van was beginning to resemble a small brothel. But when I'd finished I was really, pretty pleased with myself. Except for my fairy lights, when switched on, I discovered they were cute little snowmen, possibly explaining why they were in the sale.

My overhead cabin bed was plush. My mum had given me a perfect square of memory foam to fit on top of my solid mattress. I had fleecy sheets, a fleecy double duvet and an array of fluffy pillows. One side of my pillows sat my two favourite teddy bears on the other side I hid my big heavy claw hammer, ready to use in any given emergency. Either end of my bed housed two small windows where I hung double lined thermal curtains. In the skylight above my head I stuffed a cushion so as to prevent the entry of any unwanted beasties visiting whilst I slept. A small step ladder led up to my little haven and I tentatively climbed up to test the finished result. Milo lay on the couch, curiously observing me. Once on the top step I had to swing my right leg practically above my head and then launch my whole body onto the mattress, catching my foot in the little draw back curtains whilst doing so. I'd padded my bed with so many cushions my nose was now practically touching the ceiling. Trying to manoeuvre myself inside the fleecy sheets was like doing acrobatics in a Velcro bag, I kicked and flayed desperately trying to get comfy, inside what felt like a padded coffin, while Milo tried his utmost to try climb the ladder and join me. Once I'd settled in and looked down at Milo, now lying back on the couch having been defeated by the ladder, I thought to myself, 'this is just perfect'.

Every morning, when I woke, I'd run to the window and look out onto the street at my motor-home. My Motor-home. A home I owned. I never knew you could feel such a passion for a vehicle. But to me it was more than just a vehicle. This was my Beast. This was my future, my adventure, my journey to into the unknown. What lay ahead of me I couldn't predict, and this excited me.

But with just days left before the lease was to end on my house I was completely overwhelmed with what I still had to do. When I initially decided to do this, I thought it was basically a case of just sell everything and go. Now, here I was still surrounded by boxes and black bin bags full of 'stuff'. I also still had pets to re-home. OK, it was just two small goldfish in a small glass bowl, but they were my pets. I'd acquired them when my son had first left home for university. I was lonely. I'd named them fish one and fish two, and even taught them tricks. I taught them to follow my finger round the bowl. And they loved it. Hopefully my mum would love them just as much as I did.

I seemed to be spending hours on the phone to utility companies, writing endless emails for address updates, and filling out tedious forms for insurances, banks, mobile phones, etc.. I was doing all of this on my own because, annoyingly so, I'm far too independent to ask for help.

Deciding on which clothing to keep was so difficult for me. My three-bed semi held a multitude of outfits, shoes and handbags which I'd acquired over the years. My Motor-home provided me with one cupboard about the size of a small fridge. My decision making had to be ruthless. My mum kindly offered to store some of my clothes at her house and I managed to create a space under the bench in my van for shoes and boots. Other than that, my van wardrobe was able to accommodate about six hangers for all my outfits. I was able to adapt a shoe rack hanger to become my set of drawers, and carefully rolled all my smalls into each compartment. My main choice of clothing was jeans and jumpers, as a warm hot summer in Scotland was highly unlikely. Although I did make a point of taking one little black dress and one pair of high heels, an absolute must for any potential date.

Somehow, amidst all my chaos, I managed to squeeze in a practice night in The Beast. I chose a close to home location, packed everything I thought I'd need for one night and headed off. I'm sure Milo thought we were just going for a walk until I parked up, turned off the engine and sat on my couch. After listening to him constantly whining at the back door I eventually succumbed and took him for a small walk. On our return to the van he still persisted in whining at the door. This routine would have to change, Milo needed to learn, and learn fast, this was home. When the van stopped it was not walk time.

Later in the evening my mum and Pip turned up with takeaway food and a bottle of wine. We all squeezed around my tiny table and marvelled at how perfectly acceptable this was.

Mum then chose this occasion to have one of her 'important' conversations.

"Nicci, love, I was chatting to Pip today, regarding me ever ending up seriously ill and in hospital." Mum said.

Oh God, I thought, where's this going?

"Now, I've checked with Pip and she is quite clear on what is important to me." Mum continued "I just need to be sure you know what that is too?"

I just stared at her for a moment, wondering where all this was coming from and then suddenly I remembered a similar conversation we'd had in the past.

"Oh, Mum, I know exactly what you mean, you want me to put a pillow over your head?" I said in all earnest.

Mums face dropped. She stuttered for a moment and then screamed "Dear God, Nicci NO! I just want you to make sure my false teeth are never removed!" she spluttered. "Give the doctors a chance to save my life at least and promise me any visitors will never see me without my teeth."

"Oh, right" I said "Sorry, I just thought..."

"Yes, Nicci." Mum interrupted, "Remind me never to call you if I catch a cold."

We did have a giggle about it through the evening. And then they left. And it was dark. And I spent most of the night peeking through a gap in my curtain every time a car went past. Milo spent the night with his nose up against the back door. I was even too sacred to use my toilet in case someone heard me pee, which was just as well as I'd forgotten to fill it with flush water. I don't think either of us got much sleep that night. And we were woken rather early in the morning as I'd seemingly parked right next to a bus stop.

If nothing else I'd learnt a few lessons that night. The next day I persuaded Pip to stand beside the van whilst I had a pee, she assured me she couldn't hear a thing. All would be fine; the adventure would happen.

More from my blog miloandme6.blogspot.com

Argh! Unemployed – 29th May

Today is my last day at work...and I can honestly say it's been 12 months of hell! Contract work is not all its cut out to be. There's no safety net, no support, no recognition and certainly no end of stress. But sometimes bad decisions lead to good ones, so although I am now unemployed for the first time in my life, approaching being homeless, skint, have few friends and need to support myself and Milo surely things can only get better?!

The car booty that didn't happen – 31st May

Well today was car booty number two.   I was sorting 'stuff' out into the wee small hours and I must say it is getting more emotional.   Am now selling 'stuff' that has meaning to me, and items that I don't even own! (Son will hopefully not miss his snooker cue!). So, at midday I once again packed up the KA and headed off to the same venue as last week for a 1pm start.   But no, last week was apparently a one-off bank holiday venue and alas the field was completely empty... Milo was happy, as when I returned home to take him on his walk there was only room in the car for him to sit up front with me :)
I am now a week behind raising the Milo and Me fund so will have to get my thinking cap on for ideas.   This is my first week out of work and am feeling a little scared.

Monday blues – 1st June

Am feeling a bit down trodden today.   My first official day of unemployment and I received a 'massive' VAT bill :(Seriously contracting work is not viable unless you live at home with parents and low outgoings.   Sadly, this has eaten into my Milo and Me fund and our adventure just seems to be slipping away. I did come up with one idea last night, I am going to find a website that does swops and try see if I can swop my KA for a motor home!   Ambitious I know but God loves a trier.

Miracles do happen – 2nd June

Well I was only saying to Milo this morning that we need a miracle to happen if we are going to get this show on the road...and one happened! The Sunday Post newspaper contacted my sister Pip through the gofundme page she set up and they want to run a story on Milo and Me (looking for love). They think it is a story worth telling and asked me loads of questions about my quest to find love.   So, he is sending round a photographer to catch Milo and me at our best! And running the story this Sunday.

Preparing for the press – 4th June

Well it's nearly tomorrow, yikes! The Sunday Post newspaper are taking photos of Milo and Me for the story they're publishing this Sunday. Needless to say, I have washed my hair, chosen an outfit, tidied the house etc etc. Now Milo has just returned home from a run with his friend and as usual he managed to find every possible muddy puddle and now resembles a chocolate lab! Duh!

Am planning an early night tonight, though probably won't make any difference as I never seem to sleep well nowadays. I wake up constantly with more crazy ideas in my head so have now started sleeping with a little black note book next to my bed. Can never understand what I've written though!

I am quite nervous about tomorrow, or more so what is written about me in the publication. You always hear of people being quoted out of context. Well, for the record, I am a decent human being :) (So my mum tells me). If there are any untruths I will set the record straight on my blog. Talking of which, I am not really clued up on 'blogs' so I apologise if I don't write 'well'. I've written a diary for about 25 years and this seems similar to that.

Off to read up on the law of attraction, was told today that is what I am doing...?

The photo shoot – 5th June

Today went quite well. Milo was so well behaved I hardly recognised him! He seemed quite comfortable in front of the camera and responded to every request of him. Am thinking he could be next year's BGT winner! We took some photos of my 'stuff' ready for this weekend's car boot sale, some in the garden with a map (of which Milo did eat a page!) and then we went to a local motorhome sales office. We got to explore some of the Motor Homes and wow they are fabulous. Milo was quite at home in the passenger seat, although he did try sitting on my knee in the driver's seat! I think I have been quite spoilt seeing these motor homes as I know I will never be able to afford ones like that. But as long as I get one with a decent engine I can 'pimp' up the inside

I spoke with Ben from The Sunday Post and he informed me Milo and Me will be in the Scottish and English publication and online. Having

*lived in Perth for 10 years someone's going to think 'I know that face'!
And then probably wrap me round a deep-fried haggis ha-ha!*

Overwhelmed to say the least! - 7th June

*Oh My Gosh! I am completely overwhelmed by the amount of
encouraging and supportive messages I have received today. I am
desperately trying to respond to each and every one (and there are
rather a lot!). I really should have trained Milo on the iPad!*

*I woke up extremely early this morning and went straight online to
read my story in The Sunday Post and I must admit I did breathe a sigh
of relief... Ben Robinson wrote as if he had known me all his life! Even
more exciting Lorraine Kelly tweeted my story! My sister Pip bought 3
copies and we hung one on the car boot table! Talking of which, went
OK but only managed to raise £54, but every little helps.   Quite a few
ladies at the car boot offered me their husbands!*

*After the car boot Pip and I went for coffee and that's when we found
my story had also been published in The Mail Online and so far, that
has raised over two hundred comments! I must say most of them were
really nice (and don't worry the goldfish will be re homed) and the
yucky ones are irrelevant.*

*So, all in all today has been a little crazy to say the least.   I have lots of
new friends on social media and I am feeling even more confident that
Milo and Me will make a success of our adventure.   We certainly have
lots of people to visit on our journey, maybe one of them will be 'my'
man...*

And now the radio – 8th June

*Well if I thought yesterday was exciting today got even more exciting.
I was contacted by BBC Radio Scotland and tomorrow morning at
10.30 am live I will be interviewed by Kaye Adams. They want to talk
about my journey with Milo and Me searching for the man of my
dreams. And as I'm heading to Scotland first he may be listening. Could
be dangerous as I was once told by a previous boss that I should count
to ten before I speak! I told him that's fine, but it would just delay me
saying the same thing! (I never got far in that job). Anyway, I'm happy
to be promoting my journey and you never know it may help with my
fund and get me on my way a bit quicker. (Still not got motor home).*

*Also, today I had just got back from the beach with Milo, which was
deserted :), when there was a knock at my door. Milo did his usual
killer dog bark, and when I opened the door there was a man in a suit.*

He said, 'are you Nicci?' And I thought my word these door sellers even know your name! He then introduced himself as a journalist!! Wanted to chat to me about running a magazine story about Milo and Me.

I've had lots more lovely messages today, and one or two not so lovely. I even got a direct message asking for my hand in marriage!

I managed to get a few items advertised on gumtree and was so happy to find in a CD player my long-lost LA Freeway CD :) So have been blasting out some tunes. Now I am listening to Classic FM while I decide what to wear tomorrow...! Hey, you never know who I may meet.

Getting desperate – 9th June

Life is a bit of a roller coaster at the moment. One minute I'm walking in the park with Milo next thing I'm in a radio station giving an interview. Today me and sis did four radio interviews at BBC Radio Scotland, BBC radio Merseyside and Liverpool Radio City. And I was also contacted by various TV channels regarding filming Milo and Me. All feels a bit surreal, but needs must if I'm going to get this show on the road! Everybody was so lovely today and really put me and Pip at ease (couldn't take Milo with me!) it felt like we were just having a chat with a friend, except for the big boom mikes in front of our faces! I reckon I'd quite like to be a radio DJ.   I do hope I came across OK and not sounding too desperate!

But desperate is what I am now... I've only got about four weeks left before I'm declared homeless! And I haven't raised nearly enough for the motor home, could find myself hitch hiking around the UK with a tent at this rate!   I have contacted some reputable brand name companies today asking (practically begging) for any assistance to help my dream come true. I will make this happen, if nothing else I want to prove that anything is possible if you work hard and believe in yourself.

Positive day – 11th June

You just don't know what goes on in other people's lives. I was in a park this morning with Milo and I watched a smartly dressed, middle aged woman, on her way to work, remove an empty bottle of wine from her handbag and drop it in the bin...

Well, I've had quite a positive day. I spoke to some very lovely ladies this morning at Clatterbridge Hospital and they managed to put me in touch with an equally lovely gentleman, who is helping me with my fund raising and awareness campaign for Prostate Cancer. He is an established charity organiser for Prostate Cancer. So, watch this space for more information very soon!

I also met some super guys today, who, fingers and toes crossed, may be able to help me with the motor home. Again, watch this space for more information very soon!

I think even my mum is beginning to believe in me now...

Downbeat – 12th June

Feeling a little bit down tonight.   The day started fine, took Milo out for his morning walk and we met Pip for coffee/bone. Then I met Jen and Mel, who I used to work with, and we had a lovely catch up over lunch. But now I'm just lying here with Milo and I've got so much to do and just don't know where to start. I'm doing two car bootys on Sunday, first is a 6 am start, followed by an afternoon one.   Have checked the weather forecast and it looks like rain, which is really bad news for selling.   I've still got so much 'stuff' to sell but also still need to use some of it. I am also upset that someone left a hot disposable barbecue on the beach and of course Milo smelt the food on it and now has a little burnt nose :(

I am going to have a bath and an early night and hopefully feel more positive in the morning.

A better day – 13th June

Walking in the woods at 8 am this morning was so peaceful, until an elderly jogger decided to do bench presses on the bench I was sat on, not a pretty sight! Also, I forgot to take along Milo's ball so he spent the entire walk looking back at me waiting for me to throw it.

Came home and got loads sorted for two car bootys tomorrow.

My son and his girlfriend visited, and he gave me the OK to sell some of his 'stuff' I had.   Mind you he has had to give me a detailed explanation of what half of it actually is! Boys and their toys! And he let Milo keep his rugby ball :)

So, I've had another bubbly bath tonight (have to make the most of them, I will miss them the most!) and have set my alarm for 5 am ugh! Busy day tomorrow, please don't let it rain.

Its 10 pence for goodness sake – 14th June

Today's car boot was a disaster. Having got up at 5 am, much to the bemusement of Milo, we headed off for a 6 am start. It was heaving already when we got there, why oh why do people need to go to car boots so early?! Why aren't they in bed with hangovers? Anyway, needs must for me, so we set up our stall and sat back... 2 hours later and about 70 pence in profit, feeling frozen to the bones I'm being haggled by an old lady over 10 pence, I finally agree and she pulls a wad of notes out her pocket and asks me if I've got change! Then she has the cheek to ask me for a carrier bag.

While I was sitting in the boot of my car I saw an oil painting on the stall next to me and started daydreaming about being on the Antiques Roadshow getting offered millions for it. Daydream got the better of me, so I bought it for £2, it's a signed Burnett, fingers crossed!

Eventually after about four hours, by which time my fingers were numb, we packed up and Pip took me for a cooked breakfast. I made a total profit of £21.80... On a good note I won £5.30 on the euro millions :) not quite the 93 million, but I was pleased.

Spent the afternoon trying to catch up on my messages, I really need to keep up to speed on that. Hopefully tomorrow I will catch up with the gentleman who may be able to help me with my fund-raising and awareness campaign for Prostate Cancer. On that note I think this is valuable to know...

Symptoms can include:

needing to urinate more frequently, often during the night.

needing to rush to the toilet.

difficulty in starting to pee (hesitancy)

straining or taking a long time while urinating.

weak flow.

feeling that your bladder has not emptied fully.

Do I need new shoes? - 15th June

Received a flirty message online and I kindly quoted that I had shoes older than him, to which he replied, "jeez you need to get new shoes. I am 31!" Made me laugh. I've had so many lovely messages from round the globe it still overwhelms me.
Milo had me on the beach extremely early this morning and our usual

road was closed so we went a different route. Which was fine until I tried to follow him down a cliff, four legs are better than two, I am now sporting a rather bruised backside!

I spent most of the morning on the phone with utilities companies, the gas/electric company had me on hold for 43 minutes, luckily it was a Freephone number. Then I popped to the shops to buy 'pooh bags' for Milo and the friendly assistant recommended I buy nappy bags, 300 for 35 pence, happy days.

Thumbs up – 18th June

I keep wandering round my house not knowing what to do next, and I keep getting distracted by what I find.   Today I came across my son's new-born baby clothes and his first little black gym pumps, have to keep them :) I also have lots of blank squares on my walls where my pictures used to hang, all looks very odd.

A man offered me his camper-van today on the condition he could travel with me, I said how can I meet a man in a van with a man in the van...!   Fair Point he said.

Black Friday – 19th June

I really want to cry. I very rarely do cry. And I'm afraid once I start I won't stop. Two weeks on Monday Milo and Me are homeless. I have sold nearly everything I own. I have emptied every piggy bank. I have not spent more than a penny I needed to for so long. I have been haggled over ten pence and let down by online selling. I have been up, and I have been down on a daily basis. And it's all my own fault...

When I decided that I wanted to fulfil my dream and create my happy ending I never foresaw the emotional roller coaster it would take me on.   But I am a believer and if everything just rolled along quite nicely one would never appreciate life. I've made some super new friends and lost some. I've experienced a new appreciation of good decent people. And I've sadly learnt not to trust everyone. I've gained an important amount of knowledge into the devastating effects of Prostate Cancer, besides the fact that it stole me my father :(

Maybe today is just my Black Friday, who knows what tomorrow may bring. I will wake up tomorrow and re-focus. I will come up with a cunning plan. I will go and sell ice to some Eskimo's!

Lazy boy – 20th June

Had a good start to my day, went to buy cakes for my sister and bought a one-pound scratch card and won ten pounds:)

Waited all day again for a phone call regarding a motor home, no call :(but have seen one on gumtree that 'might' be affordable. Hope car booty goes well tomorrow, am taking my mums car so loaded up with lots more 'stuff'.

I wish there was a man in my life today, moving large wardrobes around is a back breaking task for a small single girl! So bath and bed for me now, early start tomorrow.

Father's day – 21st June

Am now concerned my budget is so low I might have to get one of these 0% credit cards. I've come too far to give up now. I don't want to be on my own. I want that special person in my life. I don't want to do everything by myself. I want to be someone's significant other! My parents had over 40 years of marriage before my dad died. Hey if I live to 90 I could have that too!

I am also getting fed up with people calling to ask if my furniture is still for sale and when I say yes, I don't hear from them again! One lady asked if I would deliver a wardrobe to Leeds (about 200 miles).

Well I've had my moan! Good news is I made £65 at this morning's car booty :)

Being Father's Day today I miss my Dad more than ever...

Things are looking up – 22 June

Just had a man in my bedroom for the first time in years... He was actually just buying my dressing table though! And then, literally 20 minutes later, I ran upstairs and threw my phone on said dressing table! Luckily not broken, just covered in the dust that was under dressing table. I also sold all my garden furniture and some bits and bobs to a lady who reconditions furniture. I seem to have more and more empty spaces in my house every day.

I also was given a really fair price for my car by local company Wirral Small Cars, they were so friendly and said would keep an eye out for any decent motor homes. I am going to see another motor home tomorrow, so fingers crossed it's a goodun, not like yesterday's!

Got it – 25th June

Hurrah! I've finally found a motor home for Milo and Me :))) I'm picking it up on Saturday, big shout out to Andy for being so patient with all my questions. So, the plan is to pick it up on Saturday and drive like a 'girl' back to mine! Then I've got 8 days to put the Milo and Me touches into it. A few family pics scattered about, a fluffy cushion here and there and create a special spot for Milo. Then we will have a practice sleep over locally and hope Milo feels at home, which I'm sure he will when I feed him in there!

This has been so stressful over the last few weeks but so worth it. My family and friends, old and new, have been so supportive I can't thank them enough. And Milo has been so patient what with all the upheaval of late. And I haven't even begun my journey yet argh!

The Beast – 27th June

Collected the motor home today, quite a beast. Just going to take some getting used to.   Handbrake on the right, ignition on the left and turn key toward you to start, plus all the other stuff! Not quite a KA! Milo jumped straight in and into passenger seat, had a good sniff round and seemed happy. Just need to spruce it up this week and make it 'home'.

Not a day of rest – 28th June

Woke up at 6am raring to go and have just stopped now at 9.30pm. Milo has had two walks and a run in the motor-home, he also got some roast beef scraps from my mum's Sunday roast. I have cleaned and sorted stuff all day. Cleared under the stairs and found some bits for the car booty, which went quite well. Came home with only one box of stuff, although I did drop some into the charity van.

I do wish there were more than 24 hours a day! Still so much to do and so little time. I'm thinking my first week away I will probably just pull up in a lay-by and sleep!

No flies on me – 29th June

I've just spent the last 10 minutes trying to flick a fly off my curtain hanging on the washing line... Until I realised it was a fake fishing fly and was completely hooked in! I don't even fish!

I was up at 6am today and have made two sets of curtains and re-covered two bench cushions with a curtain from my bedroom. Which seemed like a good idea at the time but now I only have half a curtain in my bedroom and the sun rises at 4.45 am tomorrow.

My bedroom wardrobes are being taken on Wednesday, so I 'must' finish sorting my clothes tomorrow. I put my grey bin out this morning (full to the brim) and they didn't take it, they just stuck one of those naughty stickers on it! Now I have to go to the tip.

Time for my bath now, only seven left

Three days left – 2nd July

I am absolutely exasperated at the moment and running around like a blue arsed fly. I can't believe I've only got three days left and still so much to sort. My head is a shed. My sister's boyfriend showed me how to operate things on the motor-home tonight; cooker, fridge, water, heating, gas, TV, satnav, electrics, fuses and the rest! I think it's all going to be trial and error for a while. I'm still trying to figure out the gears!

I really need to be productive tomorrow and plan my day, I also need to ask for help and stop thinking I can do everything myself. I did manage to put some bits and pieces in the van and am pleasantly surprised with what I can fit in the kitchen, although my clothes are another story...

Practice night – 4th July

I'm in my van!! OK I'm in a lay-by about 1 mile from home, but I'm in my van! Milo is curled up on sofa one and I'm curled up on sofa two. My mum and Pip have just left having popped over with a Chinese takeaway, and they took away the dirty plates too. So here I am having my first practice session and so far, so good. Although the sun is still shining and it's far too early to go to bed. And Milo did spend the first hour thinking I'd parked up to take him for a walk. And he did get a bit upset when I went into the bathroom and shut the door, he couldn't quite figure out where I'd gone!

I've just realised I'm parked rather close to a bus stop... Hopefully limited service at weekends! Milo is being the perfect guard dog and barking ferociously at everyone who happens to walk past, which pleases me. Well no bath tonight :(but will get to bed early, just hope I sleep well...

The last supper – 5th July

Well last night was fine, slept well and so did Milo. I do believe I can actually do this! I had a few hiccups! Forgot to fill toilet with water! Couldn't find drain tap for sink water, couldn't ignite fridge from gas, have a wobbly table top, didn't realise sockets don't work on van *battery, and keep tripping over the dog! But I have sorted it all and am sure I will stop tripping over the dog.*

Ben from The Sunday Post wrote another lovely article on lonely Milo and Me although I'm certainly not lonely!

I have just about cleared the house and have just had my last bath :(and my next door neighbour came round with a goodbye gift for me and Milo, so sweet.

So tomorrow I have to be out the house at 11.30 and will then head off to my local campsite for one night before I hit the road up the West Coast :) I will more than likely be travelling rather slowly, the 'beast' doesn't do speed. I also don't know how regularly I will be able to write my blog if I don't always get internet connection, hopefully it will be OK most of the time.

I went for a lovely meal with Pip, my mum, my son and his girlfriend this afternoon (probably the last decent meal I will have in a long time).

Chapter 6

And off we go

I'd done it. I'd actually gone and done it. There I was sitting in my motor-home outside the house I'd lived in for sixteen years, ready to leave.

I remembered first coming to live in this house. Having ended another failed relationship I was ready to move on. My Dad, God rest his soul, having borne six daughters was more than keen to have his grandson living near him. So he took it upon himself to find me a house close to him and Mum. I only actually saw the house the day I moved in, that's how much trust I had in my Dad. He put up the deposit and managed to persuade the landlady that a single, unemployed mum would be her ideal tenant. He even got my son enrolled in the local primary school, he was so determined to have us close by. I told myself that I'd just rent for a year or two and then get on the property ladder. Sixteen years later...

I'd just handed the house keys to the landlady and was ready to start the engine. Milo was sitting in the passenger seat beside me. He had already learnt he's not allowed to sit there when I'm driving, but we hadn't moved yet. We both just sat there staring out the window, silent. I was so apprehensive. There was no going back, yet the thought of going forward was so scary. Out into the unknown. I had everything I needed having given up absolutely everything I didn't need. All that I owned was in The Beast. Funny, I thought, how my whole life fitted into such a small space. I'd recently discovered we need very little in life, it's society that dictates we do. All Milo needed was food, shelter and love and that is what I intended to live on from now on. A friend of mine once told me that you only need three things in life; One is a warm dry place to sleep. Second is a decent meal once a day and third is someone to share one and two with. He's right! All I need now is number three.

So my journey began, key in the ignition, still forgetting to turn it towards me. 'I'm sure I'll get the hang of this choke given time, I'm sure I'll get used to the smell of exhaust fumes and I'm sure The Beast will learn to love me more than the seventeen previous owners he'd had.' I told myself.

I actually only travelled two miles down the road. My adventure began at Thurstaston caravan park, a place I'd driven past many times when walking Milo. I'd telephoned ahead and made a reservation, also choosing to purchase a Caravan Club Membership which would entitle me to discounts at affiliated sites. But as I'd never done the motor-home camp-site thing before I needed to start local, local enough that I could pop over to my mums for any forgotten emergencies.

Local proved confusing for Milo. As soon as we pulled up at the site he assumed we were on our usual walk. While I was at the reception checking in he barked furiously in the van thinking I'd forgotten him.

I presented myself at reception as if I was checking into my hotel room.

"Hello, I have a reservation in the name of Taylor" I politely stated.

"Ok luvvy, here's the site map, choose a pitch, reverse in and then come back to me for a barrier key." smiled the jolly lady.

I smiled back but inside I was crying. Did she say reverse? Why reverse? Oh how I hate reverse. I'd only reversed The Beast once and even then Pip had stood on the pavement and guided me. Milo had not been trained on this guidance.

Jolly lady must have seen the panic inside me and asked if this was my first time. I admitted it was and she very kindly offered me her husband to help me 'pitch up'.

After driving around the site a few times I found what I believed to be a suitable pitch and was kindly guided in by Jolly Lady's husband. He also showed me how to plug into the electric and made sure I was secure.

Once pitched up and plugged in I didn't quite know what to do with myself. I'd actually gone and done it. I'd given up my whole life of fifty years and here I was sitting in my new one. Milo had been walked and had quite happily taken up residence on right hand couch. I was sitting on left hand couch just staring into space. It all felt quite surreal.

'Am I a nomad, a gypsy, a traveller or just a desperate, nearly fifty-year old woman sitting in a Motor-home having just chucked her whole life away?' Then I'm thinking what life? 'A job I absolutely hated that made me cry myself to sleep every night. A social life that consisted of coffee with my sister and occasional lunches round at my mum's. A very small circle of friends who all seemed to have partners and family to consider. A rented house that I could ill afford and was never really my own home. A son who had fled the nest and settled into a successful career and relationship. And a bleak future of forever singleton, having absolutely tried every avenue to change that label'.

No, on reflection, I hadn't really chucked too much away. But I was still wearing the label of desperate, nearly fifty year old single woman. For now.

Our first morning of our new life began rather early for Milo and me. I think the extreme quite awoke us. I gave Milo his breakfast and then let him out to do his business. Then I attached him by his lead to a large iron corkscrew in the ground, a contraption I had purchased for our travels. I then busied myself making a pot of coffee. All was quiet, all was fine. Until I heard a crash of metal upon metal outside and Milo barking furiously. I jumped out the van, still wearing my pyjamas, to be greeted by the scene of Milo charging across the camp-site, dragging behind him about ten metres of red cable and the large iron corkscrew narrowly missing various vans and tents. He was in hot pursuit of a rabbit. Milo had never seen a rabbit before. I don't think the rabbit had ever come across the chaos behind him before. I chased them both, barefoot and in my pyjamas, until I got a grab on the cable. We then retreated back to the van, on the way smiling at the old man quietly sitting in his deckchair reading his newspaper with a bemused look on his face. Back in the van I cleaned up the wounds the corkscrew had inflicted onto Milo's tummy and soothed my feet with baby wipes.

We spent the rest of the day in the van. I found it curious to see all the other campers go about their business. Most of them just sat on deckchairs outside their vans, cups of tea in hand, doing nothing. We were parked near a freshwater tap and seeing everybody filling their large, wheeled, water containers I made a mental note to purchase myself one, my empty coke bottle was never going to be big enough on our travels. I drank about four pots of coffee and read a whole book. I also read the van manual as I had a flickering light on my control panel that only stayed lit if I stuck blue tack on the button below it. I made another mental note to purchase fuses. And more blue tack.

Chapter 7

It was time to leave The Wirral. Time to officially begin my adventure. We left the camp-site and made a small detour to a local camping shop to purchase a large fresh water container. I chatted with the shopkeeper and told him of my planned adventure. While paying I asked the friendly shopkeeper if I could buy some spare fuses for my van battery. He asked me what size, of which I was unsure, so I held my forefinger and thumb so far apart and said "about that big" He looked at me like I was speaking a foreign language and then proceeded to show me some examples of different sized fuses.

"Oh" I exclaimed "I have a box full of them under my driver seat, I thought they were curtain hooks."

He looked at me shaking his head with a slightly pitying look and said "Good luck with your adventure, Love."

For some reason I chose Tesco's car-park for my family farewells, probably due to easy parking spaces. Mum suggested we went in the café for a spot of lunch before I left. She was no doubt worried as to when I might eat again. So, there I sat with Philip, Pip, and Mum munching on my last supper. I made a point of saving a sausage for Milo, who was guarding the motor-home. We all chatted of my imminent departure, except Philip, he was engrossed in his mobile phone.

"Philip, will you put that phone down for once." shrieked my mum "your mum's just about to leave and you don't know when you'll see her again."

Philip looked up and gave his Nan a scowl.

"Anyway, what's so important that you have to read it now?" asked my mum

"Sorry Nan, just the French President talking about the state of the Euro." Philip replied

"Oh gosh, if it's the President of France you best reply love, your mum won't mind waiting." my mum innocently stated.

"It's newsfeed Nan." Philip sighed

"OK dear." said Nan, oblivious to all. Pip and I shared a giggle under our breath, Philip just raised his eyebrows.

In the car park we all hugged, there were no tears, we're not a very teary family, and off I went. Milo jumped onto the couch behind my driver seat and after a few miles he gently rested his head on my right shoulder, I liked that. I'd set up my sat-nav and was heading for the Lake District where I'd booked a camp-site.

Driving on the motorway was an unpleasant experience. I'd spent my whole life in the fast lane like a formula one racing driver and here I was only just managing to hit fifty mph in the slow lane. Even fifty was an effort for The Beast and incurred a loud buzzing noise from the curtain rail above my head. The Thelwall viaduct was terrifying, as I'd never driven a high sided vehicle before I soon found out how top heavy I was. Every time a lorry overtook me I felt the pull and was convinced we were going to topple over, my palms were sweating from gripping the steering wheel so tight. From there on in I let every single vehicle overtake me. My life was now always to be in the slow lane. But it didn't matter, I was never going to be driving in a hurry on this adventure.

Our night in the Lake District was fine. Other than collecting some low hanging branches via my open sky light en-route, the journey was good. I soon learnt to pay close attention to road signs warning me of bends in the road, sharp bends caused my kitchen draw to shoot out onto the floor. I also learnt three point turns in a Motor-home are near impossible and subsequently saw more of the Lake District than intended. I drove miles out my way looking for suitable areas to turn in having taken the wrong road. The camp-site was well equipped although it was so large that after our walk we spent a good twenty minutes wandering around trying to remember where I'd parked The Beast. We amused ourselves the next morning beside a beautiful lake skimming stones and taking in the scenery, but all too soon it was time to leave. We were heading for Scotland.

Our next destination was Gretna, where I'd arranged to meet a local TV news crew. This was for the Ian Payne show and they had asked if they could interview me at Anvil Hall, a wedding venue in Gretna.

This was to be my first 'wild camp' experience, as in it wasn't a camp site. I got completely lost en-route due to my dodgy sat-nav and arrived in Gretna three hours later than planned. I eventually found Anvil Hall and as having been instructed by the owner, I parked up round the back. It didn't feel exactly 'wild' as I was surrounded by houses on all sides. I did feel a little vulnerable seeing all the curtains twitching. I'm sure the residents thought I was a gypsy traveller setting up camp. My phone battery was now dwindling so I chose to sleep in my clothes that night, with my hand on my trusty claw hammer under the pillow. I also had to leave the toilet door ajar every time I entered, if I didn't Milo would bark furiously and scratch at the door thinking I'd left the van.

The interview next morning was fine, although walking down the aisle towards the camera, with a reporter, discussing the man of my dreams and me wearing tatty jeans and a jumper was a little weird. The reporter was good fun and enjoyed winding me up a little suggesting I might find Ian Payne a suitable match. Ian did send me some rather flirty messages but nothing ever came of it. The interview took up most of the morning and I was more than keen to get to my next destination. I'd arranged to visit the first gentleman on my list, Peter, in Portling.

Chapter 8

The drive through Dumfries was beautiful. I now felt like I was actually on the road. I was an intrepid explorer, I was an adventure seeking traveller, I was soaking up the wilderness of the open road. Well it felt like that for a bit, until I went through a village full of speed bumps. This is when I learnt that motor-homes literally do need to reduce down to about two miles an hour when approaching a speed bump. It was the crashing noise behind me which made me swear, definitely glass I thought, possibly crockery, maybe even my wine bottles. Thankfully it was just one wine glass and ten minutes spent positioning blue tack in all my cupboards. That was the day blue tack became my best friend.

Peter. Peter's house in Portling was gorgeous. A picture postcard house fronted by a garden so full of colour. I could see immediately this was a man who loved his garden. The grass looked as if it had been trimmed with nail scissors. Peter guided my van onto his drive and helped me out the driver's door. I opened the back door of the van and Milo came bounding out, took one look at Millie, Peter's dog, and immediately ran back into the van. Nothing I could say or do would encourage him out. Millie stood about six inches high, Milo was terrified of her.

Peter made us a pot of hot coffee and offered me the run of his house. I had a luxury bubble bath, washed my hair and even got to wash and tumble dry my clothes. His home was like one from a country living magazine. I felt it surely had a woman's influence in the décor. We sat in the kitchen overlooking the garden, Peter telling me of the work he'd put into it, me filling him in on my journey so far. Later in the evening Peter treated me to a local pub meal and then we shared a bottle of wine back at his house. As the evening drew in, although I felt comfortable in Peters company, I decided to retire to my van. I didn't feel comfortable enough to sleep in his house. And I was missing Milo.

Milo woke me at about 7am, ate his breakfast and then wandered off to the field behind the house. He returned a few minutes later looking awfully like a chocolate Labrador. He'd rolled his whole body in a cow pat and stank to high heaven. I tried chasing him with a splashing hose pipe I'd found but couldn't catch him. So I threw on my wellies and we walked down to the beach. This was my first beach in Scotland and I must say it was pretty stunning. The sun was shining and we both splashed about in rock pools until Milo's fur turned red again.

I spent the rest of the day dividing my time between Milo and Peter in the van and the house. Peter cooked me his signature spaghetti dish and opened a bottle of red wine. We spent a pleasant evening chatting, him being ex RAF me being ex air hostess we had plenty of stories to share, until he took a phone call from, I believe, the female influence of the décor. I felt like I was intruding on what appeared to be quite a personal conversation. So I took the opportunity to retire to my van, leaving a little goodnight note written on the serviette.

Peter was a perfect gentleman during my visit but alas was not the man for me. He made me so welcome in his home and invited me to return with Milo anytime. But now I was off to visit the second gentleman on my list.

Paul. Paul was only about three miles down the road from Portling in a place called Kippford. He was the manager in charge of Coastal Kippford, a private luxury chalet complex. We'd chatted online for weeks and built up quite a friendship. And in person Paul was exactly as I expected. Funny, friendly, quick witted and a perfect gentleman. He lived in a beautiful log cabin on the complex with his two dogs Duke and Ziggy. Yet again Milo was terrified of them and yet again refused to come out of the van. Paul and I spent the evening in his log cabin eating takeaway pizza and drinking pear cider. Like a man after my own heart he loved his coffee too and was the proud owner of a super-duper coffee machine. We chatted through the night about all sorts, Paul was so easy to get on with. Then, with pizza crusts in hand, I chose to retire to my van, as ever missing my Milo.

The next morning whilst Paul was at work I took advantage of his offer to use his bathroom facilities. He had one of those luxury double walk in showers and lovely selection of large man bath towels. As his home was spotless I made an extra effort to clean up after myself before heading back to the van. That's when I discovered Milo had learnt how to lock the van door from the inside. I stood at my door shivering and with soaking wet hair unable to get in. Milo was barking like mad, waiting for me to open the door. Luckily I'd left the driver window open slightly and what with The Beast being so old it had a hand operated lift up door catch that my skinny arm could just reach.

Once I'd managed to get back in the van and made a mental note to always keep my keys with me, we went off for a walk up the hill at the back of the camp-site. At the very top I had an amazing view of Galloway Forest.   I don't know how but somehow, I lost my bearings and when I came down the hill from the woods, the area seemed unfamiliar. I then realised I was in another camp-site further down the road from Paul's. It was like a maze and took me a good twenty minutes to find my way out and back to Paul's.

It was lovely being with Paul, Ziggy and Duke but I knew he was not the man for me. I could have quite happily hung out with him for longer but I'd made arrangements with another TV News crew in Ayr and had to head off. We said our goodbyes with a definite promise to return.

I didn't much rate my stay in Ayr. My satnav failed again and directed me to a cemetery. When I eventually found the camp-site, I reversed into a tree when trying to park up. I'd soon discovered how difficult it was travelling alone, I spent many a time enviously watching couples guide each other into their parking bays, usually the husband driving, the wife giving directions and positioning the chocks. Me, I had an exhausting rigmarole to perform. I had to reverse into my chosen pitch, jump out check my position, jump back in, reverse a bit more, jump out, check tree damage, jump back in, drive slightly forward, locate mini spirit level, never in the same place, figure out where the bubble should actually be, open passenger door to root under seat to find chocks, place chocks accordingly under wheels for van to be level, jump back in van and try to blindly position wheels onto chocks, check bubble, try again, check bubble, jump out of van and move chock to alternative wheel, check bubble, and eventually give up and settle for a night leaning to the left. And that's all before I've even plugged in my electric hook up cable. Other Motor-home people are always watching this rigmarole for their own entertainment. And it's nearly always raining.

While I was unravelling my electric hook up cable a couple walked by, stopped and were staring at me. I smiled politely and they approached me.

The lady then exclaimed "I knew it was you, I said to my husband, that's the lassie off the telly. Well, I think it's wonderful what you're doing, I do hope you find the man of your dreams and we will both pray for you." At which point she handed me a business card. The business card was advertising her church. Well at least I now had God backing my adventure.

The TV crew thought it would be a good idea to film me driving The Beast down to Ayr beach and find me a man. Until you own a Motor-home you don't realise how impossible it is to just jump in the driver seat and drive off. The whole setup of setting up has to be undone. Much later we headed to the beach. The beach was deserted. Except for one poor fella, minding his own business and out for his daily jog. He was pounced upon by the TV crew, camera and mic in his face, asking if he would be interested in dating me. I kind of just stood there apologising with my eyes. He nervously and politely said yes of course he would date a lady as lovely as myself. And then asked if this was actually going to be aired on TV as he was indeed a married man. We moved on. They took some footage of me walking alone along the deserted beach desperately searching for my knight in shining armour. Sad times.

My evening was spent alone, with an oven that wouldn't light, leading me to snap the door handle off in frustration. And a fuse that kept flickering on and off leading me to wedge it with blue tack long enough to boil a kettle and wash my smalls. I also slept wonky that night.

I didn't manage to watch either of my TV appearances. Although I did have a small television in my van, I could never figure out how to operate it. Most of my evenings were spent reading books, or in sheer exhaustion going to bed early. But I loved this lifestyle, all the stress my body had previously endured: the headaches; the back aches; the teeth grinding, they'd all gone now. I felt peaceful.

Chapter 9

The next day we left Ayr and I spent the next couple of nights staying with my best friend, Sue, in the town of Perth, where I used to live. It was a lovely catch up with Sue and she was more than enthusiastic about my adventure. Sue and I had become best friends over twenty-five years earlier when our sons had attended the same nursery school. We were both single mums then and were both parenting the naughtiest boys in the class, it was destiny we should become friends. Over the years we experienced all the highs and lows of life together, Sue was always there for me and I her. And throughout our friendship, a pot of coffee, sat at the kitchen table, always seemed to cure any problem we had. Today was no different.

"Do you think I'm mad, Sue?"

"No madder than the rest of us, Nicci." Sue replied

"You've had so much shit thrown at you over the years, Nicci, but you always keep smiling." Sue continued, "you have so much strength and courage and now you're channeling it to your advantage."

"But what if I fail, Sue? What if I don't get my happy ever after, I don't want to return with my tail between my legs." I wept into my coffee cup.

"Nicci, you listen to me and you listen hard. Everybody has dreams, ambitions or goals. But most of us don't even say them out loud let alone attempt to accomplish them. So whether you succeed or fail, you are to me, and anyone else who matters, an inspiration. So, you keep going and you enjoy every minute of your adventure because you deserve it."

"I love you, Sue, any more coffee in that pot?"

A few days in Perth with Sue was the recharge I needed, now I was ready to continue my adventure. It was time to meet the third gentleman on my list.

Andy. Andy lived in East Neuk. He'd given me directions when we'd chatted on-line and he wasn't too far from Perth. I found his home quite easily, Devil's Lodge. An aptly named house with little stone Devils perched on the outside of the building which was quaintly shaped like a fifty pence piece. His home was at the entrance of a large estate. On arrival he instructed me to park my van just beside a large area of burnt grass. He informed me that only two nights ago his car had caught fire in the night and was destroyed. The only evidence remaining being the patch of burnt grass, which I dubiously parked beside.

I was quickly introduced to Rebus, his dog, which of course resulted in Milo diving straight back into The Beast. Then I was given the tour of his home. Unlike Peter and Paul's homes his was, as I expected a man living alone to look like, untidy and full of man clutter. It was homely though and held an abundance of character. He told me to take a seat on the couch whilst he made coffee. I managed to find a small space free of trash at one end and was immediately joined by Rebus. I watched Andy rummage through the sink full of dirty dishes looking for cups. After coffee we took the dogs down to the beach and Milo, quite happily swam with Rebus. On our way back, we stopped at the picturesque harbour in Elie and bought fresh crab for our supper. That evening Andy presented me with an impressive meal of dressed crab, home grown new potatoes, whole beetroot and poached egg. It was absolutely delicious. We then sat on the couch with Rebus and watched a boy type DVD. After finishing the bottle of wine I retired to the van, cuddled up to Milo, climbed my ladder and fell asleep.

I stayed at Andy's for two nights and he was the perfect host. But I knew, yet again, he was not the man for me.

I was now three men down and feeling slightly disheartened. They were all perfectly decent men in their own different ways and had plenty to offer a girl. But there was just something missing for me. I couldn't put my finger on it and certainly couldn't describe it but was sure I would know it when I saw it or felt it. People kept asking me what it was I wanted in my perfect man so I drew up a 'small' criteria description:

Physically

Tall or at least four inches taller than me. His eyes will be his main feature, they will draw me in with his every look. His hair will be any colour but there will be enough of it to run my fingers through. Body hair is fine as long as it's not a carpet back. No tattoos would be good also, no jewellery other than a watch, which he will always remove in bed. His body will not be skinny, his shoulders will be broad, his belly may have a small pot to match mine. His upper arms will be strong enough to lay my head on at night. His thighs will be those of a rugby player that will enable me to dead leg him with my elbow when he winds me up. His hands will be manly and clean, with a gentle touch. His bottom will be the cutest thing in my world, but not as cute as mine...

Personality

He will ooze confidence with an air of arrogance that he has earned. He will be intelligent and know words that have to be explained to me without making me feel stupid. He will have an organised mind but will be able to throw caution to the wind at a moment's notice. A funny man who always gets the hidden joke. Warm and kind hearted but won't suffer fools gladly. He will know his strengths and yet recognise his weaknesses. He will be honest enough to admit another lady is beautiful but faithful enough not to stray. He will be able to read me like a book without revealing the end...

Status

His employment will be important to him. His salary will afford us a luxurious lifestyle but will not be the most important detail in our relationship. He will come from a large and loving family who will welcome me with open arms. He will have a wide and varied mixture of friends who will become my friends also...

Us

He will always be attracted to me and me him. We will always respect each other's space. We will love each other unconditionally. We will have a mutual trust but both will always have the insight of reasonable doubt. We will strive on a daily basis to work on our relationship without excluding the outside world. And most importantly, he will love my Milo...

Personally, I didn't think I was looking for the impossible.

Extracts from my blog miloandme6.blogspot.com

Left the Wirral – 8th July

Milo and Me actually left the Wirral today! Having had two nights at Wirral Country Park Caravan site which is about two miles from where we lived. We are now in The Lake District, therefore no Mum, Son or Sister popping in with items I'd forgotten to buy or just sitting with me having a cuppa. No this is real now. We really are on our own. In the woods. Miles from civilization... OK there are hundreds of other campers! But I don't know them, yet!

Need a holiday – 9th July

What a crazy 24 hours. No internet connection last night, hence no blog. So yesterday I left the Lake District and headed for Scotland. I arrived at Gretna after getting a little bit lost in the lakes as my satnav packed up on me. The lanes were so narrow and windy I think I brought a few tree branches with me! I arrived at Anvil Hall about three hours later than anticipated and parked up in a very lonely car park with no power.   I cooked a slightly unfresh pasta meal and watched the charge on my mobile quickly dwindle. I slept in my clothes just in case!

Heath, the owner of Anvil Hall arrived at 9am and kindly let me charge up my mobile and iPad and gave me a tour of Anvil Hall. It is quite stunning and if I didn't have my heart set on a wedding in Italy I would choose Anvil Hall. Matthew from ITV Cumbria arrived at about 10am and we filmed the interview to be broadcast on the Ian Payne news show. It was a strange experience. But Matthew was lovely and put me at ease.

I then left Gretna and headed along the coast towards Portling (stopping off at Sweetheart Abbey) to meet Peter and his dog Millie, my new friends.   Millie is about 6 inches high and Milo is terrified of her and will not leave the van! Hopefully I can persuade him to come to the beach tomorrow. I am staying here for a couple of days and will sit down tomorrow and plan next week's route, I hope! I am exhausted and feel I need a holiday...

And the adventure continues – 11th July

I am still in Portling in favourable company! I've had a bath, washed my hair, washed my clothes and even had them tumble dried! I've got electric hook up and internet connection all is good. I will be sad to leave I've been so spoilt. But my journey continues. I am travelling towards Ayr tomorrow and have booked a site through The Caravan Club.

Milo has spent most of the day in the van again as he is still terrified of

Millie, although he did brave up and approach her in the garden this morning.   I took Milo to the beach and he absolutely loved it, we stayed for about two hours.   This evening I was presented with a lovely home cooked meal and a glass of Pimms by my new friend Peter. And he even helped me put the blocks under my van wheels so I can sleep horizontally tonight!

This adventure is providing me with oh so good days and oh so what have I done days...

How to pee quiet – 12th July

So, I left my friend's house after a lovely two days of a little luxury, and travelled a total of three miles to my next destination! So I'm now settled in Kippford for one night and have received a lovely welcome. Milo has sort of made two new friends, Ziggy and Duke, and has zonked out on the couch after a long walk in the woods. I'm thinking this really is Scotland's Riviera Coast, the scenery is just stunning and the beaches are wonderful.

My friend provided takeaway pizza and pear cider, just lovely. And we spent the evening chatting about our beloved dogs :) Now I'm settled in my van but it seems the neighbours are having a bit of an outdoor party, and I'm sure they can hear me pee...!

Washing my smalls – 13th July

One night at Kippford Holiday Park was not enough so hopefully I will return one day. The Dumfries area was an excellent choice to visit and meeting Peter and Paul was worth the visit, true gentlemen.

So now I am in Ayr for one night. I am being filmed by STV news tomorrow morning...! The drive here was fine until my satnav kept telling me I had reached my destination at a cemetery. I took Milo for a walk down by the river and of course he jumped straight in, add the rain and now I have one very wet dog in my van, urgh! I tried to cook chicken nuggets in the oven tonight but it kept blowing out and I got so frustrated that I ended up pulling the handle off the oven door! Then the fuse to heat the water kept disconnecting so I had to stick it with blue tack, which didn't work for long so I had to boil a kettle to wash my smalls!

Bath time – 14th July

Yeay! Have arrived at my best friend Sue's house for a well-earned rest! Am now in Perth for a couple of days (my old home town) and feel quite at home.   Milo has settled in well and has found a comfy spot on Sue's couch, after eating the contents of her bin! Sue gave me a tour of her massive house and I gave her a small tour of my van.

This morning STV news filmed us at Craigie Gardens Campsite and we drove down to the beach to chat to the locals. Although most people were not local and were there on holiday. We left Ayr with a temperamental satnav which only kicked in after about 10 miles, luckily going in the right direction. I must get used to this slow driving, the only vehicle I passed today was a JCB and even that was tough uphill towards Perth. Milo was the perfect passenger and either watched out the window or slept on the back seat, I do wish he could drive the van!

Had a lovely FaceTime with my son and sister, which rather confused Milo. And now off to have a big bubbly bath.

Van separation – 15th July

Last night I slept in a house for the first time since leaving and it felt strange. I think I've got van separation issues! I had a lovely long hot bath and fell into bed at about midnight. I'd found a bottle of cocoa *butter cream in the bathroom and thought it would be nice to smother my face in it... So did Milo!   This morning I've taken advantage of the washing machine and Internet connection. Oh and the Tassimo coffee machine :)*

So after catching up on three loads of washing I took Milo into the town centre. Not a good move, he doesn't much like traffic and did his dead dog impression part way down the high street. After gently persuading him to move we arrived at the park. I didn't know there was a pond full of ducks.   There weren't many ducks left once Milo had taken a running jump and belly flopped in! He then did his shake off the water move just next to a family sitting on the grass enjoying the peace and quiet. Fast exit to the furthest point away after profusely apologising.

We then met my best friend Sue for a coffee and wandered around the shops whilst she was in the hairdressers. Not much fun for me as not allowed in most shops with Milo, I did contemplate wearing dark shades and pretending he was a very badly behaved guide dog! I was allowed in one shop, Mountain Warehouse, where I purchased a micro towel half price :)

Was quite depressed meeting Sue out the hairdressers looking all glam and me looking like I've lived in a motorhome all week...

Short and sweet – 16th July

Am so very tired now. Just eaten, just caught, fresh today crab, had wine and watched dvd American Sniper. All in all a good evening. Milo is crashed out after swimming a marathon with Rebus, his new friend. So I am now climbing the ladder to my much awaited bed...

Today will be tomorrow – 18th July

*I have decided it is probably wiser to write my blog the day after 'the'
day... But this blog is today! And I will write about today tomorrow!
And I've already written about yesterday so I don't really have
anything to write... Confused? I am! Basically I will write tomorrow
about what I have done today. Just hope I can remember it all :)*

*I am still enjoying myself. It is hard work moving around all the time
and fitting in with certain restrictions. I also can't believe how quick
the time is going. And I can't believe how many different baths and
showers I've had! I've been fortunate enough to have met three perfect
gentlemen so far, who have all treated me like a lady (my sister Pip is
probably laughing out loud just now). I've been wined and dined and
had some truly good conversation. Milo has also made some lovely
new friends. But my journey continues...*

Wild camping – 19th July

*So I left The Devil's Lodge in East Neuk yesterday and headed to
Dunkeld.   Yet again I forgot to flick on my car battery, every day I
forget something, oh and I forgot to top up water supply. Satnav went
on strike again, but luckily I am familiar with the area. And, yet again
I had a small army of cars trailing behind me as I trudged up the
Perthshire hills!*

*I arrived in Dunkeld about midday and headed to a recommended car
park by the river. I was intending to park for the night but the swell of
the river and the forecast of torrential rain persuaded me to move on. I
found a lovely secluded car park behind the cathedral and set up camp.
Milo and Me then headed into the town and came across a salmon
tasting event at Dunkeld Smoked Salmon, delicious. Then we headed to
The Taybank pub (dog friendly as on walking in Milo jumped straight
up to the bar and placed his head and two front paws on the bar and*

was served a dog biscuit) I had a bottle of beer and free use of the Internet. Lots of people stopped to admire Milo and we had a lovely evening chatting to various people. Milo eventually fell asleep at my feet so we headed back to camp.

The car park was empty except for us which was OK during the light. Then it got dark so I put Milo on 'bad guy watch'. I woke up at about 3am with the torrential rain which was made worse by the fact we were parked under a big tree. It was like someone dropping stones on the roof. Eventually I couldn't stand it any longer so fired up the engine and moved away from the tree. Got back into bed and lay for ages wondering if I'd switched off my headlights... Got back out of bed to check and I hadn't!

This morning we had a long walk through the woods by the cathedral before heading off to our next destination...

Need to buy a hose – 20th July

We left Dunkeld early yesterday and headed for our next destination Killin.   I was quite impressed with the 'beast' as it only took us just over an hour. It was a lovely quiet drive and we only had one car stuck behind us. It did get a bit hairy scary at one point when a big coach came towards us on a very narrow stretch of road. We had the Loch and a steep slope on our side, the coach stopped to let us pass and I honestly didn't think we'd get through. I had to open the window and pull in the wing mirror and edge through whilst breathing in! The trail of cars behind the coach were practically applauding!

We arrived at our site and checked in. We stopped at the water point to fill up and there was no hose just a tap. I just stood there like a numpty wondering how to get the water into the tank. Apparently I'm supposed to carry a hose to do this but there has always been one on the tap previously.   I ended up borrowing one from a friendly motorhome neighbour :) talking of friendly motorhome people I have discovered that when on the road all the other motorhome people wave to you! Trouble is my eyesight is pretty rubbish and I keep waving at random white van drivers!

We set up camp and walked into the village to buy supplies, stopping off for a coffee in a little cafe. I stupidly bought bags of shopping forgetting I'm not at Tesco in my car and had to walk all the way back to the van with Milo and heavy bags. Arms like lead when we got back.

Later we went for a walk down past the cemetery, that was a little boring! So, we headed on through the woods down a track. We headed further down this long, long track not knowing where it would end up until we got to a clearing and found Loch Tay. I love walking in the woods, there is 'always' something beyond the woods worth seeing...

As it was Sunday yesterday I cooked a lovely meal. Got two pork steaks and took them outside and battered them in a bag with my big claw hammer on the van step! Then slow cooked them with yummy gravy and mash, had two helpings so good :) and Milo got the scraps

Chapter 10

We kept on travelling north in a zigzag kind of fashion, stopping at various locations including Dunkeld, Killin, Oban, Invergarry, Loch Ness, and Brora. Every day brought another stunning view be it the greenest of a field, the rugged edge of a mountain or the sky reflected so clearly in a loch. Milo spent most of our travelling time seated behind me with his head on my shoulder, he was also fascinated with what he saw.

Our day to day life had now formed an acceptable pattern. It was a pattern I liked as it could be changed at a moment's notice. Our days began around 7 am. I swear Milo could 'hear' my eyes open. I wouldn't hear a peep from him all night but as soon as I opened my eyes he would let out a little whimper. I'd peep over the side of my overhead bunk and see him on the couch below, big sad Labrador eyes willing me to feed him. So, our day would begin with Milo's breakfast, followed by my pot of coffee. I kept Milo's dog food in a large sealed container stored in the foot well of the passenger seat. This area was now classed as our conservatory and the dog food container was my coffee table. We'd both sit there most mornings taking in our daily view. If we'd wild camped our view was usually stunning, if we'd booked a camp-site our view could be stunning or it could be a toilet block. Late morning we'd head off for our next destination, making a point of sourcing a supermarket for food supplies, as village shops charged extortionate prices and my daily budget was meagre. My fridge was so tiny, food was best bought on a daily basis. Since I'd broken my oven my meal choices were mainly stews or a cooked breakfast, anything that could be cooked in a pan on the stove top really. Milo didn't care what I cooked as long as he got the leftovers.

When we wild camped we tried to be discreet. We tried to find locations that were not imposing on the neighbourhood. We never stayed for more than one night and certainly never left any trace of us being there. In fact, I often picked up other people's litter rather than anyone think I had dropped it.

Our afternoons always involved exploring wherever we were. Walks in the woods, exploring beaches, skimming stones on lochs, outdoor café stops, window shopping in town centres. I did miss out on certain activities as invariably it was 'no dogs allowed'. But I'd rather miss out than leave Milo alone in the van. After my evening meal Milo would curl up on his couch and I'd curl up on mine, with a book to read. And bedtime always came early. All safe and sound in our Beast. Life was good.

Brora, a favourite location for Milo and Me. Our camp-site, Brora Caravan Club, was right on the beach, once we'd crossed the local golf course. The site wasn't too big and yet afforded us plenty of privacy. It was immaculately presented, and the facilities were top notch.   Also, the weather was in our favour, no rain.   It wasn't quite bikini weather, but the sun was certainly shining for us. Our beach, and I say our beach as we had it all to ourselves, was spectacular. Miles of pure white sand lapped by the clear water home to a family of seals. Or were they otters? I'm not too clued up when it comes to wildlife. Chucking the ball for Milo I could have been throwing him into a swarm of sharks. It's not even a swarm is it? That's bees. Maybe it's a school, or is that fish. Whatever! I watched those cute creatures bobbing their heads up and down for about an hour and Milo never got too close anyway. We stayed on the beach until the sun started going down and the temperature dropped slightly. Before we left I grabbed Milo's ball chucker stick and carefully wrote 'MiloandMe' in the sand. I positioned my phone on a rock, set the ten second camera delay switch and ran to sit on the sand next to my inscription. Milo always follows me when I run so my reckoning was he would be in the photo too. He was. He sat on the word 'and'. About half an hour later and about twenty photograph attempts we headed back to the van.

Brora Beach

Back at the van I cooked a big pan of Scouse with crusty buttered bread. Our Motor-home pitch backed onto a farmers field and I had a lovely view from my kitchen window whilst I washed the dishes. I even spotted the farmer, on his tractor, ploughing the field. I went off into a daydream then, imagining me as a farmer's wife. Husband out working on the land all day, me in my big kitchen cooking him a hearty meal for his return. Domestic bliss. I waved to the farmer but he was now just a mere dot on the horizon and a memory in my imagination.

This was a good camp-site because it had Wi-Fi. I struggled on a daily basis while travelling without Wi-Fi. My blog was basically written as and when, more often than not in local pubs and cafés. But that often meant leaving Milo locked in the van. There are quite a lot of establishments that do allow dogs inside, but Milo is not the best behaved where food is involved. He would have the sandwich out your hand in the blink of an eye given half a chance. So we tended to avoid places serving food. Tonight though I had decent Wi-Fi. I decided to contact gentleman number four. As my satnav had broken I was now relying on maps. I wasn't sure if we were nearing his location so I sent him a message telling him where we were.

Mr P. Dear Mr P, was, it appeared, only about an hour away in Watten. Little did I know but he had it in his head that I wouldn't reach his part of the world for at least another month. And here I was telling him I would be there tomorrow. Mr P lived in Watten which is in Caithness. I knew nothing of Caithness other than the glass. But he gave me clear directions on how to find him, which included bends in the road, steep hills and clusters of trees. Not quite satnav but I duly wrote all this down.

Extracts from my blog miloandme6.blogspot.com

My magical castle - 21st July

This malarkey writing the next day about yesterday is frustrating me so am just going to write as and when I can. I have only got 38 minutes of Internet connection as the site I have just arrived on has no Wi-Fi! So, I trudged to reception to enquire and the lady said just walk one mile to next village and the little café is open until 8.30 with free Wi-Fi. Was more like 3 miles and not a single pavement on the way. Saw a lot of smashed wing mirrors in the ditch and could only assume they hit some poor pedestrian like me! I am staying at Oban, right on the beach at North Ledaig Park. The drive from Killin was pretty spectacular. The views over to the islands are stunning and Milo has been in the sea already. It is a very open site and I do feel a bit like a goldfish in my van! I am going to attempt to get a bus into Oban tomorrow with Milo, that will be a first for both of us!

Stressful bus journey - 22nd July

Am possibly having my first low point so far, which is not bad as been travelling few weeks. We are sitting in MacDonald's car park in Fort William using their free Wi-Fi. The campsite we planned to visit is full so not sure where we will be tonight (possibly still MacDonald's!).

Last night was a bit dull. When we left the café we took a short cut back to the site along the beach, was much nicer than walking on the road.

Back at the van we had no internet, no TV, no friendly neighbours and a helicopter overhead for nearly two hours! Milo is terrified of helicopters and hid under the driver seat most of the night. I did manage to use the laundry facilities and even tumble dried stuff. I then read some maps and went to bed.

This morning we had a lovely walk on the beach and then caught a bus into Oban. Milo was so well behaved for his first bus journey :) We had a walk around Oban and a quick coffee before catching the bus back. On the bus back Milo couldn't fit on the floor by my seat too well so he sat on the seat next to me. He was very quiet and very still but a man came up to me and said I should be bl**dy ashamed of myself! Then the man behind him said he was an arrogant b***d and to ignore him! Then the lady behind him said of the second man he had got it the wrong way round! He then basically told her to shut up! Don't think I'll be travelling on buses again, too stressful.

Before we left Oban, David from The Oban Times newspaper came to visit us to write a piece in his paper. He told me they have over 40,000 readers so possibly one could be my Mr Right! Well I think I'll move on 'cause Mr Right ain't in Macdonald's car park...

Yesterday, before we left Killin, we went for a walk in the woods by the camp. We stumbled across what I can only describe as a derelict castle, it was quite magical, but alas no Prince Charming...

We spent most of the day in the van as it rained constantly, I did get some 'housework' done though.

Have to stop writing now as café closing and getting bitten to death by midges!

Get the bikini on - 24th July

*I think I've found my favourite campsite, Brora, right on the beach :)
am going to stay here forever!*

*We ended up sharing our lovely little lay-by in Invergarry with two
other late night arrivals, they were a bit noisy but we didn't complain!
We left the lay by in Invergarry and just started driving North, didn't
even realise I had passed Inverness until we had passed it! Before we
knew it we were beside Loch Ness, it's massive. My driving is getting a
bit better, even managed to overtake a big truck! Stopped off in
Evanton and had a bowl of soup in the van and gave Milo a quick
walk.*

*Then we arrived in Brora, the campsite is lovely and we got a great
spot right next to the golf course. When we walk to the beach we have
to look right as we cross the course! The beach is stunning, could be in
the Caribbean if it were warmer, though the sun has been shining :) we
practically have two miles of coast all to ourselves, Milo is loving it.
Had a pleasant evening, watched a dvd (when I eventually figured out
how to work it!) When I was washing the dishes I saw a rather good
looking farmer on his tractor out the back window, was tempted to say
hello but he drove off into the sunset...*

*Went back on the beach this morning and also did some hand washing,
must remember not to try hand washing jeans again, hard work! Now
sitting in a pub (drinking coffee) just to get Wi-Fi! Then heading
towards Watten to visit a friend.*

Chapter 11

The next day we headed off to Watten, stopping off at a pub to post a blog entry. Mr P was absolutely right in his description of the route. The bends in the road were hair raising. Berridale was an eye opener for The Beast. The incline was about 14% on the road sign up and down. Hairpin was an underestimation and made all the harder without power steering. Going uphill I was lucky to get into second gear, downhill had curious 'crash lanes' which freaked me out a bit. The queue of traffic behind me just kept building up but I didn't care, I just wanted to get out of this alive and not end up over the edge of a cliff.

We eventually hit some straight road and took a left at Latheron Wheel as instructed. Then it was a good few miles of flat open moorland scenery blotted only by ugly wind turbines. I had an idea we were not too far from his house and for some reason decided to stop in a lay by. Out of the four gentlemen this one had me feeling a bit nervous. I didn't know why, there was no difference in my routine. But I sat in the lay by for a good twenty minutes contemplating. Think positive I told myself, 'Feel good in yourself and portray that'. Then I chose to brush my hair, spray some perfume and slap on a little lippy. And off we went.

I knew I was nearing his house, I could see, in the distance, the cluster of trees on the bend he had described. Although Caithness had forests full of trees, apparently, I later found out, planted in the eighties as some kind of rich man's tax benefit, there were very few, what I call, old trees. I believe that is probably why there are so many wind farms, so much open space.

Unfortunately, as I neared the trees I hadn't slowed down enough to turn in and having a car up my backside I had to drive on past his house. It was a few miles before I could pull over into a garage forecourt, turnaround and head back. I was now approaching Mr P's house, not on my right as instructed but on my left, and my heart was in my mouth.

I pulled into his turning and stopped in front of the big wide gate. There was a cute sign on the gate saying, 'dogs at play'. I sat there for a moment gazing up the drive. I couldn't see the house, all I could see were trees, very big and very old trees. But I could feel the presence of the house, I could feel it beckoning me. I jumped out of the van and opened the gate towards me, unfortunately I'd driven too close to it and had to get back in the van and roll back slightly. At this point I regretted not wearing my wellies as I squelched through the muddy fallen leaves in my suede ballet pumps. I drove through the entrance and then had to go through the whole process again on closing the gate. About a hundred yards up the tree lined drive, I came to a roundabout of manicured lawn in front of the house, the house took my breath away, so much so that I forgot the Highway Code and turned right at the roundabout.

The house stood there before me, big and proud looking. It was an extremely old, grey stone-built house and appeared to make a statement looking out over the land. The drive went the whole way around the house and was in turn wrapped by more manicured lawns. To the front of the house was a magnificent, if not slightly tired, walled garden. The walled garden sloped down towards a small lake with the brae running up behind it. Just above the walled garden I noticed a flagpole, flying the Scottish flag.

I parked to the side of the house, switched off the engine and jumped out of the van. Mr P appeared from the back of the house and walked towards me, smiling. I liked what I saw. Mr P had a thick head of dark floppy hair, he had beautiful, piercing blue eyes and nice teeth. He wasn't as tall as I like but he was taller than me. He was wearing a crisp white shirt, sleeves rolled up showing strong tanned arms. I had a gut feeling his tan ended at his elbows. On top of his shirt he wore a navy-blue gilet. His jeans were slightly baggy and, on his feet, he wore gumboots, unfastened. He stood, rather intimidatingly so, just staring at me and puffing away on an electric smoker's pipe. This reminded me of the old cowboy and Indian films I used to watch with my dad, I'm sure someone, somewhere was reading these smoke signals. In my nervousness I launched myself, through the smoke clouds, at Mr P and threw my arms around him.

"Hi, I'm Nicci." I squealed nervously.

"Well, it's a pleasure to finally meet you, Nicci." he said in his soft, slow and extremely posh accent.

Milo, at this point, came bounding out of the van barking ferociously. That is until he spotted Tessa, Mr P's dog. Here we go again, I thought, as Milo darted back into the safety of the van.

Mr P guided me through the garage and into the kitchen. I noted the garage doors where electronically opened and a couch was positioned facing out towards the roundabout. Once in the kitchen Mr P instructed me to take a seat and offered me coffee. I took the only seat available, a tall bar stool situated beside the kitchen island. I asked him why he only had one stool and he said he'd only ever had the need for one.

I looked around me, at the large bright kitchen and marvelled to myself how wonderful it was. The main focus was a grand black Aga built into a large alcove at the far end. The kitchen units were all new but sympathetic to the style of the house. They were a warm butter colour with light wood unit tops. Behind me stood a large dresser with leaded glass doors housing various knick-knacks. The kitchen accommodated five doors in total, one from the garage, one leading down a hall into the main house, one into the breakfast room, an external door to the rear garden and one taking a small staircase up to the maid's quarters. There was no maid.

Two large windows gave me a picturesque view onto the fields behind the house. I could also see a strange shed type building, upon my enquiring, Mr P told me this was where he housed his falcon. Mr P then spoke, for what felt like hours, about his love of falconry. It was in his blood. It was what his whole life was about, as his father's before him. Unfortunately as I knew absolutely nothing about falconry I could only um and ah throughout this whole conversation, not at any point mentioning my fear of birds.

Once we'd finished our coffee, Mr P suggested we take a tour of the grounds on his quad bike. We left the kitchen through the garage and he started up the quad, instructing me to jump on the back behind him. I then found myself straddled behind Mr P not quite knowing what to do with my hands. I decided to hold onto the seat pad behind me, that is until he suddenly revved forward and I instinctively wrapped both my arms around his waist to stop myself falling off the back. And off we went, down the lane and up the brae, me wrapped around him like a long lost lover and feeling quite at home.

We headed down towards the gate at the entrance but hooked a sharp right over a quaint little stone bridge, Mr P informing me this used to be the original old road. Our quad then climbed the steep brae, so steep thus causing me to grip even tighter into his waist. Milo, who had chosen to follow us, was barking furiously and trying to get his teeth into Mr P's gumboots. We finally reached the top of the brae and parked up next to a curiously placed picnic table, there was no picnic. Mr P beckoned me to sit down and take in the view. Behind me lay the loch in its full glory, Mr P pointing out his little red boathouse in the distance. And there in front of me stood the house, looking even grander than before. To me the house had the presence of an important old lady. She stood so proud looking and in complete command of the walled garden below her. She was surrounded by trees as if they were family members protecting her existence. The lake below shimmered her reflection and the sunlight bounced off her windows like smiling eyes. I absorbed this image for a long moment all the while feeling like my grandmother was hugging me. Mr P was watching me. I believe he knew how I felt.

When we returned back towards the house I caught sight of my van and noticed a compartment door was slightly open. Closer inspection revealed it was the door housing my van leisure battery, minus the battery!

"Oh no!" I screamed "my battery has fallen out"

"I don't think batteries just fall out, Nicci." said Mr P.

"When did you last see it?" He asked

"It was there this morning when I unplugged at the camp-site." I cried. "Maybe it fell out on one of those crazy bends."

But like Mr P said, I surely would have heard or felt it and it was securely strapped into its housing. I could now see the straps were just dangling, unbroken but neatly undone.

"I've been robbed!" I shrieked like a true Scouser.

Mr P just smiled calmly and assured me he knew a man who could quite easily sort me a new battery in a day or two.

"Don't worry, Sweetie," he said, "this just means I get to enjoy the pleasure of your company for longer whilst we sort it out."

Hmm, I wondered. Had Mr P enlisted a battery thief whilst we were on the brae?

Later that evening Mr P prepared us a roast lamb dinner with leeks and new potatoes whilst I sat on the stool watching. He talked endlessly and

I listened. Before serving dinner Mr P offered me the use of his bath, knowing how much I missed this activity. On route to the bathroom he gave me a tour of the rest of the house.

The kitchen corridor led to the main hall of the house. On the right was the breakfast room with a small wood burning fire, a comfy looking couch and the breakfast table. Off to the left was his study housing a large desk under one of the windows. Mr P pointed out a space he had cleared for me, at the large antique desk, for me to do my writing, with my own desk chair opposite his desk chair. 'How considerate and thoughtful' I thought. We then headed into the dining room, the central focus being the biggest dining table I'd ever seen, there was room for sitting at least twenty people quite comfortably. A huge ornate chandelier dangled above. This room was so grand and had large, ceiling height shuttered bay windows overlooking the walled garden. We left the dining room, passing the large front door incorporating what I call a porch, although this porch was bigger than my van and housed a humungous mirrored dresser and an umbrella stand full of ornate walking sticks. Adjacent to the front door was a WC, again bigger than my van with one wall covered in hooks holding all Mr P's coats. We continued down the corridor and arrived at the drawing room. This was another grand room overlooking the walled garden and filled with three large, white, comfy sofas. The big and imposing fireplace crackled away, spreading warmth through the room. This room was double aspect, overlooking the walled garden and another view to the side of the house. A door to the rear of the drawing room, now a drinks cupboard, had originally led to the butler's pantry. There was no butler.

We left the drawing room and headed up the grand staircase, passing a big bay window on the turn. I stopped at the window as I could see my van parked outside, I peered out and saw Milo, sitting in the passenger seat, staring out of the window, and a little sadness came over me.

I was then shown all the bedrooms the last one being, Mr P said, mine. This room overlooked the walled garden and beyond to the loch. It had two big shuttered windows. At this point I had realised none of the windows had curtains, only shutters. There was a Victorian style sink in the corner of my bedroom and a beautiful fireplace with an enormous oak framed mirror above. The bed was an ornate, dark wood sleigh bed covered with the softest white duvet. Laid on the bed was a selection of white fluffy towels and a similar robe. On one of the bedside tables was a water jug, a crystal glass tumbler and a tub of very expensive looking body lotion. I also noticed, placed on my pillow, was a gold wrapped chocolate mint.

"Oh, my word!" I exclaimed "I've checked into the Ritz."

"I just want you to feel at home, Sweetheart." Mr P whispered.

Home. I don't ever remember my home like this. But I'm sure I can get used to it, I thought.

I was shown to 'my bathroom' and Mr P headed back downstairs to continue cooking.

I started to run the bath at which point Mr P returned with a glass of champagne for me to drink whilst soaking in the tub. I joked that I felt like I should be bathing in the champagne not drinking it.

I lay in the bath, champagne in hand, the aroma of minted roast lamb wafting under the door, and contemplated my situation.

I liked Mr P. I liked him quite a lot already. He ticked a lot on my tick list. Maybe it was time to step indoors, as in step out the van. Yes, I decided, I would sleep in The Big House tonight, as I had now christened it.

Milo and Me at The Big House

Chapter 12

The next morning, after an extremely peaceful night's sleep, I awoke to a small strip of sunshine creeping through a gap in the shutters. Milo was curled up on a blanket at the foot of my big sleigh bed, having been persuaded with copious amounts of biscuits to follow me into The Big House. I lay there for a while listening to nothing. It was so peaceful. I then put on my big white fluffy bathrobe and headed down to the kitchen.

I eventually arrived in the kitchen, having been used to just stepping into it in the van, and there was Mr P amidst a big cloud of pipe smoke handing me a hot mug of milky coffee. He then gave me a big hug and kissed the top of my head. Mr P was a very tactile person, I am not.

I then noticed what looked like my knickers, folded very neatly, on top of the Aga.

"Erm, are they my knickers on the Aga?" I enquired.

"Yes, Darling, I took the liberty of emptying your laundry from the washing machine. You now have the hottest knickers in Caithness!" He giggled like a schoolboy.

I was just grateful I had chosen to launder what I believed were my decent knickers.

The next few days were spent exploring Caithness. Mr P was full of knowledge and passion for the surrounding area. Our days were filled with visits to historic land sites and meeting neighbours. Mr P would enthusiastically introduce me as the wonderful lady he'd discovered in the Daily Mail newspaper and how lucky he felt that I had chosen to visit himself. I was taken to all of his favourite childhood places, where he'd spent his summers learning about Falconry from his late father. We visited salmon runs and hidden freshwater pools for Milo to swim in. We spent days driving around counting the ugly wind farms blighting the landscape with Mr P sadly telling me of many a falcon being sliced in the blades.

Mr P had sourced a new battery for my van and as the garage was on the road to John O'Groats I decided to take Milo with me and make a day of it. I had planned to travel to Orkney but having to spend over a hundred pounds on a new battery funds were tight. So, a day trip to John O'Groats was a good substitute. Other than take the obligatory photo under the road sign there wasn't much to do at John O'Groats so we headed back, taking a Milo stop, at Dunnet Head beach.

Heading back to the Big House I had to stop for petrol. I could see the petrol station up ahead on my left and indicated to turn. The problem when you're driving a motor-home is all the other drivers. They seem to make irrational decisions when they spot you on 'their' road. Like the one coming towards me now. He obviously decided I was going to take days to travel the few yards ahead and chose to cut right in front of me. Braking sharply in a motor-home is never a good idea and usually incurs most of my belongings to bolt forward. On this occasion breaking sharply caused me to take the turn into the petrol station awkwardly and on approaching the pump I hit the kerbside. Trying to manoeuvre forward I felt something on the side of my van scrape something else. In my panic I just carried on driving forward and straight back onto the road home.

Back at the Big House I told Mr P of my mishap. We checked my van and I'd mangled some sort of air vent on the passenger side. But I was more concerned of what damage I might have caused to the petrol pump.

I had visions of it having blown up on my departure, causing untold carnage. Mr P suggested we take his car and drive over to inspect.

Fortunately, the petrol pump was shielded by a large metal construction and there was no apparent damage. Only to my poor Beast.

One lovely sunny day, Mr P suggested a trip to Dunrobin Castle. Mr P was very good friends with Andy, who on a daily basis put on a spectacular bird of prey display in the grounds of the castle. I got to get up, close and personal with one particular falcon in Andy's kitchen. I don't know how I didn't run out screaming as I still hadn't mentioned my absolute fear of birds to Mr P. I think the fact that this bird was wearing a little hat covering his eyes and was so still he could well have been stuffed helped me hold my own. On leaving Dunrobin Castle we stopped in Golspie for fish and chips and ate them in the car on the beachfront. Milo sat in the back drooling like a running tap. Heading back to Watten, Mr P took me on a detour to Latheronwheel harbour, a little hidden gem, down a steep and narrow lane that I wouldn't have known about otherwise. Milo loved it here, jumping straight into the water and then running up and down in the long grass on the cliffs. It was such a lovely spot, we were the only people there.

Back in the car I saw a cute little money spider on Milo's head. I gently encouraged it into my hand and showed Mr P.

"Aw look, I have a little money spider in the palm of my hand." I told him.

"Darling, that's not a money spider, it's a tick." Mr P informed me.

After an hysterical performance by me involving much jumping up and down and a lot of itching and twitching we headed off to the pet shop to purchase a suitable tick treatment for Milo and a lesson for me in tick recognition and removal.

Our evenings were spent with me watching Mr P cook roast dinners, always with leeks and new potatoes and listening to all of his stories. Mr P encouraged my ritual of hot bubbly evening baths, always supplying me with a glass of fizz. Before bed he always placed a hot water bottle under the duvet for me and every morning I was greeted with a big hug and a mug of milky coffee. This was always followed with toast, never without the toast rack, a choice of jams and a proper butter knife. I'd never seen a toast rack without it being stacked with mail.

Even Milo seemed quite at home, once he'd accepted the fact that Tessa was extremely old, slightly blind and only growled if he got too close.

Mr P had a habit of always wanting to hold my hand, be it crossing the road or even when I was just sitting on the stool in the kitchen. I wondered if I would ever feel comfortable with this. I loved being in his company, I did find him attractive, but I wondered if his tactile nature may suffocate me. Also, Mr P wanted to talk. To talk constantly. He never stopped talking. He seemed to want me to know everything about him and basically opened up his soul to me. Mr P had a haunted soul. Mr P wanted me to know this. This endeared him to me.

After four nights staying with Mr P I realised I had to make a decision. Mr P had made it quite clear he wanted me in his life.

As he said "What's mine is yours, I would be the happiest man alive to share my life with you."

I was happy with Mr P in The Big House, as was Milo. But I'd made a decision to go on an adventure, to travel the West Coast of Scotland, and to meet the man of my dreams. Had I met him already? Should my adventure end now? Had I, in all honesty, found my happy ever after? I wasn't sure. I had a niggling doubt it was not here. But I also had a fluttering feeling that it could be.

But, and a big but, we hadn't even kissed yet.

On my last night I lay soaking in the bath with my flute of champagne in hand contemplating leaving tomorrow without ever knowing. Yes I found him attractive, yes I enjoyed his company and yes I knew he wanted to enjoy me. But I could hear my mother's voice in my head "don't sleep with him if you want him to respect you." My main thought though was 'it's a long way to travel back to find out'. Therefore wouldn't it make sense to find out now, before I left. It's all very well him saying he didn't want me to leave and he prayed I would return. But what if I came all the way back and we just didn't click, sexually. Surely it made sense to just sleep with him tonight and leave tomorrow, knowing.

I decided to telephone Pip, already knowing what her advice would be. And, as I guessed she agreed I should just 'do it'.

I stepped out of the bath onto the deep, soft white John Lewis bath mat and wrapped myself in the fluffy white John Lewis towel. All of Mr P's linen appeared to have been purchased from John Lewis, of this I approved. I smothered myself with the tub of expensive body butter, the one Mr P had kindly placed beside my bed on my first night. Then I put on the extremely large white, John Lewis bath robe and brushed my hair. A quick check in the mirror and I grabbed my empty champagne flute and headed downstairs to the drawing room. Where I grew up we called it the lounge, but then again, we didn't have a dining room, a study, a breakfast room, a butler's pantry or any of the other various rooms spread over the Big house.

Mr P was sitting on the big white couch by the roaring log fire. He smiled at me like he knew all my bathroom thoughts. I looked at the other two white couches and sat myself next to him, curling my bare feet under me. He graciously refilled my flute, without filling his own, Mr P drank very little alcohol.

He took my hand, as he so often did lately and stared right into my soul. He spoke of his sadness of my forthcoming departure, yet knowing he had no right to hold me back. He said 'he admired my spirit and understood my need to travel'. He respected I had an unfinished journey and requested just one thing from me. That I would return to him. 'What is mine is yours, what I have I desire to have with you, I would be honoured to share my future with you.' he told me again.

Mr P then said he had a confession. Apparently since the first day he had met me, four days in total, he had felt the most intense pain deep inside himself. He had not felt a pain like it since he was a teenager. He explained this was an unbearable yearning to feel himself within me. I had awakened him from years of nothing. I had restored in him a feeling of utter pleasure. His pain was an absolute throbbing in his groin that only I could satisfy. But, he then went on to say, that being the gentleman he was, he would under no circumstances take advantage of a lady like myself. He had an utter respect for me and was willing to bear this pain forever, rather than sully me with his advances.

I sat there in a state of disbelief and bemusement. Quite frankly, I told him, any normal man would have at least pleasured himself to alleviate this pain. Or words to that effect...

We sat there for a while, with only the sound of the logs crackling in the fire. The full moon rose on the brae and the rooks had started to descend into the trees. I couldn't quite decide how to react to Mr P's confession. So I referred to a recent story he had told me about. One where he had fallen foul of a relative and had spent many, many years storing up so much anger and hurt but without unburdening it. He had then, after many years, written to this relative explaining his pain and told me he had immediately felt relief.

I asked him how long he was willing to wait for me?

He took my face in his hands and kissed me, passionately, for what felt like forever...

The remainder of our first sexual encounter resulted in the tried and tested fumble. I was obviously already naked under my robe, he had to endure the removal of all clothing. I politely didn't watch and kept my eyes closed, only for a moment opening them to witness his tan evidently did end above his elbows and below his neck.

Our passionate encounter in the drawing room was to be our only. Every other sexual encounter would be experienced in the bedroom, under the duvet, in the dark. Except our last...

After Sex...

Having made sure the fire was out and the doors were locked we both headed upstairs. I was curious to know why Milo had not disturbed our encounter in the drawing room. I soon found out. Milo was curled up on my bed, the contents of my handbag scattered around him and an empty, chewed up bag of dog treats under his chin, not to mention a whole packet of tissues shredded across the duvet. I just wanted to hug him.

Mr P said it would give him the greatest joy to wake up next to me in the morning. I couldn't give him this pleasure. I'm a bit odd like that. I'd spent the evening letting him explore my whole body but I wasn't ready to actually sleep with him. I asked if he'd mind awfully if I slept in my own room with Milo and he graciously agreed. We all slept well that night.

The next morning Milo and me left to continue west on our adventure in The Beast. I felt it was right to leave Mr P, even after our night of passion. I just wasn't quite sure about him, it had all happened so early on in my adventure, it seemed a bit too good to be true. I needed to keep travelling and reflect on all so far. Mr P held me so tight when we said goodbye, he told me he understood, he hoped we would return but if we didn't he was grateful he had spent this time being with me. He then placed a Saint Christopher around my neck and prayed I'd be safe. And off we went.

Extracts from my blog miloandme6.blogspot.com

Second disaster - 26th July

So I'm lying in a hot bubbly bath with a long, cold vodka and tonic whilst the minted leg of lamb slowly roasts in the Aga... And to be honest I deserve this after today...

This morning started well.   I woke with the sun peeping through a slit in the shutters and came down stairs to a hot milky coffee. Milo and Me set off with map in hand to find Dunnet Bay.   When we arrived the sun was still shining so off came the wellies and socks and I let my toes see summer for the first time since my journey began :) We stayed on the beach for a good two hours playing ball and admiring the coast line. Then we decided we were too close to John O' Groats to not visit. So off we headed. We got the tourist photo at the sign post and sent a postcard to my mum. Met some friendly tourists and had a little walk around. Soon it was time to head back and that is when my next disaster occurred....!

I was really low on fuel so decided to stop at one of the extortionately overpriced petrol stations. Not only are they overpriced they are very short on space! Unfortunately my back end got stuck on some kind of metal guard and in a panic I drove forward, thus removing a large chunk of my side rubber edging and part of my gas vent cover!

Seriously I am not going to have much van left at this rate. I was so embarrassed I drove away on empty. Mr P and I returned later in an unmarked car to check for property damage and cctv...! None of the above. I haven't read a paper for ages but can imagine some local headlines 'cyclist found in ditch with leisure battery embedded in his head' 'Caithness fuel station shut down due to idiotic English female motorhome driver'

Mr P took me for a drive around the stunning area of Caithness which is only spoilt by the bloomin' stupid wind turbines...!

Salmon run - 28th July

Lazy day today. Got up late, well 7.30, which is late in my world. Had coffee, bacon and eggs. Sat around for most of the day procrastinating, knowing that I had to sort out my battery situation. Eventually late afternoon I took a trip up to the local agricultural garage, whom I had phoned earlier, to purchase the battery. The mechanic said it looked as if had been stolen as no damage to door. He then tried to fit new battery and after a few electric shocks had it installed and running!

Went for a little run back to Loch More and took a photo of the salmon run, very impressive.

We ate a great meal this evening at the Ulbster Arms in Halkirk with Mr P's friends, very pleasant. Came back to lovely mug of hot chocolate.

Spoke to my mum this morning and she questioned me as to why I had hot knickers and what had I been up to?!! Explained to her that they were literally airing on the Aga...!

Birds of a feather - 29th July

Not such a lazy day today. Sort of went back on myself and took a run out to Dunrobin Castle, which is back near Brora where I stayed last week. Quite a stunning building with fabulous gardens and a beach for Milo :) I got to meet Andy who does the Falconry display and even though all who know me know how terrified of birds I am, I sat through the whole display and loved every second of it, I learnt so much. I had a walk through the gardens and then had coffee and smoked salmon on toast with Andy and his wife.

On the way to Dunrobbin Castle we stopped at a lovely little harbour in Latheren Wheel and had a walk around for a photo opportunity. And on the way back from the Castle we stopped for fish and chips in Golspie.

Probably not going to get to Orkney the price is working out at £110 return and after spending £105 on a new battery funds are low. So now just planning a route around the west coast.

Ticktock - 30th July

Whoa up late! 8.15, must have been tired. Had a lazy morning then went off exploring on the moors and found a lovely pool in the river.

Came back through Wick, took some harbour photos and some of the old ice stores.   Then went to Campster and saw the old burial mounds. Now to me they looked like a delivery of gravel for a new drive, but apparently they are stacked quite appropriately, according to Mr P! Back in the car, heated seat on of course, and had a yummy steak pie from the butcher, 'Bews' who used to supply The Queen Mother, delicious!

Now in my last bath with a glass of champagne and to then sit down and plan my route for my departure tomorrow. Milo and Me won't know what's hit us when we get back in the van...

Chapter 13

I'd only driven about an hour when I saw a hitch-hiker. He looked so young and vulnerable standing on the edge of the road in the rain and I felt sorry for him. He made me think of my son, and if that was my son hitch-hiking I'd want someone like me to pick him up, a mum person. So I pulled over and watched him in the wing mirror grab his bags and run to the passenger door. As soon as he opened the door Milo barked and growled like a mad dog. The poor boy stood there terrified as I explained Milo was just saying hello. My hitch-hikers name was Michael, he was seventeen and from Holland. His family were very proud of him taking time out of school to explore the world before university. With The Beast struggling up the hills, the hairpin bends and Milo's head resting on his shoulder I'm sure Michael wondered if he'd live to ever see his family again. Michael got out at the next town, I'll never know if that was his intended destination. Milo and I carried on toward Tongue.

That night, we wild camped next to a cemetery on the Kyle of Tongue. It truly was the most peaceful location so far and obviously our neighbours were very quiet. The sunset was a superb photo opportunity arched with a glorious rain shower rainbow.

The next, morning I was woken by the sound of the morning tide lapping lazily beside the van door. When I opened the door Milo literally jumped right in and had a swim. I brewed a pot of coffee and I sat on my back step absorbing the tranquil atmosphere. This is the life I thought.

We then headed towards Kinlochbervie on a long and winding road. The road snaked through the landscape always giving you views miles into the distance. There was little traffic, often we only shared the road with random sheep, who always had right of way. Every twist and turn brought another 'wow' from me as I absorbed the vast landscape. As usual I'd forgotten to secure everything, this time it was the kitchen cupboard shooting open and the contents spread everywhere. It made me think back to my air hostess days. I flew for ten years and quite often I would forget to secure something in the galley. As crew we were all quite adept at sitting in our jump seats on take-off or landing with various arms or legs holding a trolley door in place. I couldn't do this in The Beast, what with me being the pilot. And Milo, as my cabin crew, had never learnt to intervene these disasters. I think he was just hoping at some point it would be the fridge door flying open. Maybe I should have adopted the 'cabin secure for take-off' rule with Milo.

We stopped off at a beach in Durness for a Milo break. When I opened the door, Milo shot out before me and headed down the steep cliff towards the shore. By the time I got to the cliff edge he was already on the beach and aiming towards two ladies, sitting on a blanket, with what looked like a picnic. I hurled myself down the cliff, running and screaming his name. My legs were going faster than I could handle and I nearly went a cropper. I managed to steady myself just in time to see Milo running off, down the beach, with a whole Victoria sponge cake in his mouth. The ladies just sat there opened mouthed watching Milo devour the cake. I apologised profusely and ran with Milo towards the far end of the beach. When I decided that we were far enough away I sat down on a rock to get my breath back. That's when Milo decided to go back for seconds. As he was running back towards the picnic I could see the ladies desperately trying to grab all their food before he reached them. I then had to run back to them and again offer my apologies, this time trying to give them money for their lost food.

"Oh God, I'm so sorry, please let me pay you." I shouted breathlessly.

"Nine, nine." one lady replied.

Flaming heck, I thought, nine quid for a cake, that's a bit steep.

Until I realised she was German.

They had refused my cash donation and chosen to pack up and leave. We now had the beach to ourselves and Milo was well fed.

We arrived at our camp-site, Clashview, in Kinlochbervie and I chose a spot looking out over the cliff. On arrival I'd noticed a sign near the entrance saying storm refuge parking and wondered what it was for. I found out during the night. I was woken up with a vigorous rocking sensation and instantly regretted our choice of pitch. The storm was vicious and I was too scared to get out of my bunk let alone move the van to the storm refuge parking. So I just lay there riding the storm and praying I wouldn't be found bobbing about in Loch Clash or the Atlantic Ocean the next morning.

The next morning arrived, the sun was shining and the birds were singing. I was alive and still parked up on the cliff-top. Our little camp-site housed no more than five pitches and one fresh water tap, but it was the stunning location we were paying for. A lady in the van next to me informed me we were permitted to use the shower facilities in the harbour. I could see the harbour below us in the distance, certainly not within walking distance. So, we packed up the van, placed our £15 in the honesty box and drove down to the harbour.

After much wandering around, looking for a sign indicating shower facilities, I knocked on the harbour masters office door to enquire. The harbour master kindly took me round the back of the building, along the quayside, past the fishing boats, through a building as big as an aircraft hangar, and there, in between some forklift trucks was a little door with a picture of a shower upon it. Inside were rows of lockers with large yellow, rubber fisherman outfits hanging on the doors. Big fishermen boots lined the floor and a whiff of fish hung in the air. I stood there with my little pink fluffy towel under my arm wondering if today would be a good day to 'not' take a shower? But the harbour master had left and I was alone. I nervously opened the door to the one and only shower and peeked inside. It was a rather basic shower and possibly not the cleanest I'd come across during my travels. There was maybe just enough room inside to undress and hang my clothes over the door without the shower spray soaking them. As I stood, lathering up under the hot water thinking 'this isn't so bad' I heard voices. I tentatively peeped through a slit in the door and saw about half a dozen big hairy men donning the fishermen outfits. My shower lasted longer than I'd planned as I waited for them all to leave before I dared to creep out. Unfortunately, although I'd hung my clothes out of the showers reach I'd omitted to position my boots accordingly and had to squelch back to the van.

The rest of our day was spent on the beach at Oldshoremore, an absolute favourite for Milo and me. We could well have been on a Caribbean beach, miles and miles of golden sand, coves with hidden rock pools, the water so clear like glass, and the sun beating down on us. Milo did his bouncing lamb impression as soon as he hit the sand. He always did this impression when he approved of our location. He did this impression a lot on our travels. It was so hot that day and as the beach was deserted I stripped down to my underwear. Luckily, I've always been a matching underwear kind of girl, 'just in case'

After our glorious beach day our journey had us heading towards Ullapool. This is when we picked up our second hitch-hiker, Martin. He was from Germany and unlike Michael, he wasn't scared of Milo, or my driving. He spent his time peering around my van and I decided he was staking it out for a robbery-stroke-murder. When we got to the next village I pretended we were staying there and therefore had to drop him off. As soon as he'd grudgingly got out of the van and closed the door, we sped off and kept going. I drove for about another hour and then found a nice spot near a river to camp over-night. The next morning, we actually saw Martin at the side of the road, thumb out, smiling broadly. I dropped a gear, revved up some speed and flew past him hoping he didn't recognise us. No more hitch-hikers I decided.

Ullapool was grim for me. Milo found a dead fish on the beach and first he rolled in it and then he ate it. As the tide was out I had to walk him about a mile out to try and rinse the dead fish smell from him. And that night, whilst I slept, he puked the whole dead fish up on my carpet, twice. I spent most of the next day on my hands and knees scrubbing the carpet, trying to remove the pungent fish smell.

The next couple of days were an improvement. I'd booked into Inverewe campsite right on the edge of Loch Ewe. This was such a good campsite I booked it for two nights.   I'd stopped on route at the Aultbea Hotel and whilst chatting to some local men at the bar, they had invited me to a Ceilidh they were organising in the local hall. Alcohol, men and entertainment, things were looking up. Not. It was basically a room lined with plastic chairs and a space in the middle to perform the highland dance. Small children and grannies seemed to be the popular choice of dance partner as the band played out. I stood in the background observing and recalling the one time I was involved in an activity like this. It was Hogmanay, I was living in Scotland and was attending a dinner dance. Full of alcohol I convinced myself I could join in with the highland dancing. Unfortunately my high heel shoe caught in the hem of my long black evening dress as my gentleman partner flung me round the room. I returned into his arms on one foot with my thumb indicating down my back towards my stuck foot. He just thought I was re-enacting that scene from the movie, Airplane and continued to twirl me around until I fell into a heap on the floor. Battered and bruised I swore I'd never highland dance again.

The band had now announced the buffet was being served and as I was swamped by a scrum of bodies I snuck out the side door and headed back to my van. It had been a pleasant evening and I'd been made to feel very welcome but I was tired and feeling a bit lonely. Back in the van with Milo curled up on the couch, I realised I was missing Mr P. He had telephoned and messaged me every day since I'd left and I liked that. But, I decided, I had to keep going. My adventure was onwards not backwards.

After another couple of nights wild camping we were now aiming for Skye. One of our wild camp nights had been so wild I didn't even know where I was. I'd stopped on the road side and not a single car passed by through the night. The silence was quite deafening and the only sign of life was a small herd of sheep trotting down the road. When darkness fell, and it truly was the darkest night I'd ever witnessed, I became rather scared. I couldn't see or hear anything outside and didn't want to switch my lights on in the van, thus drawing attention to the obvious murderers hiding in the hills. I was even too scared to sleep in my overhead bunk, remembering an old horror story about a zombie creature on the roof of the car, which would certainly break through my skylight and drag me off into the hills. So I slept on the lower bunk with Milo, fully clothed, keys in the ignition and held my claw hammer and torch all night. I actually slept quite well considering.

My next mishap occurred at Applecross. Not being the best map reader I headed in a sort of straight line. This in turn took me on the Bealach na Ba mountain pass. Apparently this road is compared to similar roads in the Alps and takes you to the highest point of the U.K. Oh boy! Once on that single track road there is no turning back. It got steeper and steeper reaching 20% inclines. It twisted and turned and The Beast struggled even in first gear. Worst still was meeting another Motor-home coming towards me. Sadly, I was positioned on the outside of the narrow track. He pulled into a passing point where we both pulled in our wing mirrors and he beckoned me to pass. At this point, edging forward, I burst into tears as I felt the road crumbling down the mountainside under my wheels. A few cars had now queued up behind him and I swear they all did the cross sign as I inched forward. Milo sat behind me with his paws covering his eyes. On seeing my tears the oncoming Motor-home graciously chose to do the inching forward as I just held my breath and joined Milo in covering my eyes. When he was eventually clear of us the row of cars all cheered and gave me a thumbs up. I then breathed out.

Going down was no better. The 20% incline was now a 20% decline with the same hairpin bends and the added fear of brake failure. But at least I now had the mountain on my side of the road and an amazing view of flat land in the distance. Once off the mountain I pulled into a lay-by and grabbed my map. The Beast had done us proud but there was no way I would ever drive The Beast over a mountain again, it was now the time to learn how to map read.

That night we found a safe and non-murderous wild camp spot near the bridge to Isle of Skye. After a decent night's sleep, we headed off and crossed the bridge to Skye. These are moments I wished I had a co-driver to take photographs, the ones on the road when you can't stop. I wondered if I could train Milo on this? I'd read about assistance dogs that could do laundry and the like so why not operate a camera?

I headed to a camp-site I'd written down and after a few wrong turns eventually found it. Unfortunately there was no availability for me. I must have looked quite disheartened as the lady in charge went out of her way to suggest some alternative local overnight parking. My closest options were the whisky distillery car park, if arriving after 6pm, or the local cemetery at any time. Although the whisky distillery sounded appealing I didn't want to wait so I headed to the cemetery. Sure enough it was a lovely spot, very quiet and surrounded by fields. Once I'd parked up and made a pot of coffee I went to let Milo out. Unfortunately a calf had escaped from the neighbouring field and was wandering round the car-park hotly pursued by his rather large and intimidating mother. They remained in the car-park with us until much later that evening when the farmer arrived and guided them back into the field. I was dubious as to how secure they were and made the decision to keep Milo in the van. Milo had a face like fizz all night.

To add to my misery the next morning I ran out of gas. Mid coffee brewing. Now I had a face like fizz. I then had to drive miles out of my way to find a place that could not only sell me a gas bottle but fit it as well. I'd stupidly not learnt how to do this and didn't even have a spanner. When I finally found a gas supplier they informed me the bottle I was carrying was illegal and I would have to professionally dispose of it and buy a new one. More miles out of my way. More pennies out my budget.

I'm sure the Isle of Skye has a beautiful landscape, unfortunately I didn't see much of it. It rained. It rained constantly every day. The dark cloudy skies followed us all over the island. I did find a camp-site with availability but I stupidly chose to do a laundry load using the camp-site washing machine, that was all well and good but there wasn't a tumble dryer. I had to hang all my clothes throughout the van and blast them with my hair-dryer, all the while hoping I wouldn't blow any fuses.

Next morning I packed away my damp clothes, which had attracted a family of midges into the van overnight, and headed off the island.

Back on the mainland, tired, disheartened and with a face full of midge bites I checked into a camp-site with full facilities. I had decent Wi-Fi and sent Mr P a message full of my sorry tale.

Mr P sent back a short reply.

"Come home, darling"

And so, that's what we did. Milo and me went home.

Extracts from my blog miloandme6.blogspot.com

Michael the hitchhiker   31st July

Well I've left Caithness with a heavy heart and a St Christopher... I had just a perfect week and saw and learnt so much of an area of Scotland I knew nothing about. I met some lovely people local and not local. But now my journey continues.

I have reached Sutherland and made a pit stop in Tongue after dropping off my hitchhiker...! I know, jeez Nicci what you doing?! But he reminded me of my son and I felt sorry for him... His name was Michael and he was from Holland. He was travelling like myself only 30 years earlier than me! Anyway I do believe I have a good judge of character and I feel he was more fearful than me when he stepped into The Beast! The roads are single lane most of the way with random passing places and hills so steep we had to lean forward! Milo rested his head on Michaels shoulder for most of the journey, no doubt peeved Michael was blocking his view!

Rainbows and hot chocolate - 1st August

How lucky are Milo and Me?! Found an absolutely stunning location last night on The Kyle of Tongue. A little spot just next to the water and no neighbours for miles.   It was next to a grave yard so very peaceful too. I think I sat on my back step for hours just taking in the scenery and absorbing the tranquillity. Then we had a rain shower followed by the most beautiful rainbow on the horizon. Just chilled out for the evening reading my book and eating buttered crumpets.

This morning I awoke to the sound of the tide gently lapping the shore. I opened the door and Milo jumped out and went for an early morning dip. The sunrise was as stunning as the evening rainbow. I didn't want to leave, I sat in the sunshine for a good two hours before I tore myself away to head for Durness.

I tell you, if you ever want a stunning drive then travel the A838 it's amazing territory. The road is mostly one lane with an abundance of 'passing places' and the rugged coast line views are to die for! Every twist and turn in the road brought another 'wow Milo look at that'. We arrived in Durness and took a walk on the beach in the pouring rain and now I am treating myself to a rather yummy hot chocolate at Cocoa Mountain :) then off to camp down for the night.

A handsome highland cow - 2nd August

We arrived at Kinlochbervie and pitched up at the site. Our one and only neighbour pointed out the beautiful wild orchids growing next to my van. She then recommended we visit Oldshoremore beach and am I glad she did! It was the steepest road The Beast had encountered so far, but so worth it. It was so warm and sunny (and practically deserted) that I stripped down to my underwear and had a little sunbathe! Milo swam in all the lagoons and ran for miles on the sand. We had a fab *afternoon. I decided to take about 36 selfies hoping that potentially I would have one photo of me that I actually liked... I now have about 36 photos of me that I actually quite like! The Beast did struggle back up the hill and could only manage in 1st gear...that is until I realised I still had the handbrake on!*

We stopped off to photograph the most handsome highland cow I'd seen so far :)

I am now in a local pub having a bottle of beer and using their Wi-Fi, the pub reminds me of the film American Werewolf in London! Beware the moon Nicci...

The fish van - 5th August

For anyone out there thinking my adventure is all a bed of roses... It ain't! Had a rather depressing 48 hours with one thing and another.

Sunday night in Kinlochbervie was scary, there was a terrible storm and I had stupidly parked 6 foot away from a cliff! Woke at 4 am rocking and rolling! And now realised what the sign 'storm refuge parking' meant!

Monday morning I decided to use the site shower and laundry facilities... Only 1 mile away in the fishing harbour, rather strong smell of fish and full of Captain Birdseye lookalikes! But need's must.

Continued our travels along the west coast picking up another hitchhiker, Martin from Germany. He was a bit boring so we dumped him in Lochinver. We travelled for another few miles then decided to wild camp next to a beautiful fast flowing river. That was fine until about 2 am at which point I wanted to scream 'turn that blooming river off'! We left that spot (which I don't actually know its name, possibly near Inverkirkaid) early morning and took a rather scenic route on the A835 towards Ullapool, passing Martin the hitchhiker on the way! Gave him a friendly wave!

Ullapool seemed nice so we booked into a campsite on the shore. Bad move. Milo found some kind of dead animal on the beach and ate it :(even worse he brought it all back up some hours later on the carpet, twice! I now have a van that stinks of rotten fish. Oh and he rolled in the dead fish before he ate it so he stinks too! Also it rained all afternoon and we were stuck in the van most of the day, and I had bought fish cakes for my tea :(The site had advertised Wi-Fi, but oh no, not where I happened to park. I walked to two local pubs last night and still couldn't get on the Wi-Fi so gave up and returned to van to read my book and absorb the aroma of fish...!

I am a little happier now, the sun is shining in Aultbea. I am in the Aultbea hotel enjoying a coffee with some new friends who have invited me to a ceilidh this evening...!

Recommended - 8th August

Can't believe I've been travelling for over a month now. I would recommend this experience to anyone. I think I've only had a handful of down moments, which in my previous 'life' would have been so many more. And a down moment usually consists of spilt coffee or a wet dog, not too much to complain about!

Found a little second hand book shop in the village this morning and got myself two more reads. My usual choice of a gruesome murder, keeping my imagination active when wild camping!

Isle of Skye - 10th August

Funny, I used to think luxury was a five star hotel, nowadays it's a campsite with a half decent shower! Having just spent the last 3 nights wild camping I'm splashing out tonight at the Torvaig site in Portree Isle of Skye. I've got electric, water, laundry, hot showers and Wi-Fi! Although I am may be regretting the laundry as no tumble drier but having got electric my hairdryer will run all night!

Having safely got off the mountain on Saturday I stupidly took a wrong turn and had to backtrack for an hour, then I seemed to be driving forever trying to find a 'non murderous' spot to wild camp. I eventually found a lovely quiet picnic spot near Kyle of Lochalsh (another cliff edge but plenty of trees to break my fall) and settled down. During the evening many other people followed my example and I woke up to a make shift campsite! One large motorhome had blocked me in and I had to wait for him to leave. We left our spot and headed for the bridge to Isle of Skye. Just before we crossed the bridge I purchased petrol at £1.23 thinking it would be even dearer on Skye, no first garage on Skye was charging £1.15!

How to turn it on - 11th August

Seems to me that every house on The Isle of Skye is a bed and breakfast! Never seen so many, not that I'm a snob...but even some of the council houses ran b&b's. Didn't get to see much more due to the terrible rain and poor visibility, the sun shone for about an hour before we left. Had to flick the hair dryer back on the washing this morning, all still damp. Managed to even blow dry my hair, though kept hitting the ceiling with the brush, oh the struggles I have living in a tin box!

My midgy bites on my face are now making my eyes itch (SSS not working!) so we only drove for about an hour and are now camped in Morvich, on a site, oh boy more luxury! I actually feel happier back on mainland. I think I'm getting a dab hand at manoeuvring the van. Makes me smile when I see wives guiding their husbands into spaces making a meal of it, and all I do is launch my head out the driver window whilst reversing with one hand like a truck driver! Although I'm not sure what route to continue with tomorrow as I am terrified of taking the van up another mountain, and I bet even a grown man would have cried doing my last mountain experience!

Milo still has some travel issues. He still cries when I use my bathroom. He still can't figure out a kissing gate. He still thinks he can cross a cattle grid. He still wants to watch the whole journey over my shoulder. And he still jumps up on the bar at every pub.

For some unknown reason I seem to have attracted a fair amount of Twitter followers from the music industry and mainly from Canada?! I have no idea why, unless they think I'm some sort of Scottish pop star!

Well I am going to try and work out my TV tonight, only been over a month and I still haven't figured out how to turn it on...

And they lived happily ever after - 14th August

I am going off radar for a wee while... I can't/won't say too much just now as I don't want to jinx myself, but you'll never guess what?!... I believe I've met someone special :)

He will be reading this (hi x) so I will write accordingly! I met him a few weeks ago, he read my story and invited us to visit him. So we did. Then we left and continued travelling. But two days ago I realised I missed him terribly so drove all the way back. And I don't know at this point if we will ever leave...! And I know he doesn't want us to.

So that's my story so far. 'Approaching 50 Jobless Boyfriend less and Homeless' was my story so two out of four ain't bad.

Less than two months ago I decided to live out my dreams. I was so scared and aware it could all go horribly wrong. Some people believed I was crazy (they are probably not far off the mark) but I believed in myself for the first time in my life and I'm so glad I didn't change my mind. I would say to anyone that has a dream, go for it. Don't worry about 'what if's', don't worry about what other people think and don't talk yourself out of it.

Maybe this is my Happy Ever After...

Be back very soon with update and any printable juicy gossip!

Chapter 14

Back at the Big House and straight into Mr P's arms. Even Milo ran into the house. And straight to Tessa's food bowl.

After a big hot bubbly bath and one of Mr P's roast dinners, we curled up on the couch in front of the big roaring fire. Mr P held me so tight in his arms, I certainly felt like I was home.

That night I crawled into my big sleigh bed with Mr P, who had slept there every night since I'd left, and we fell into a blissful sleep.

We had a wonderful few days getting to know one another properly but all too soon Mr P had to fly down to London on business for a few days. It was unfortunate but couldn't be helped. I drove him to the airport and then headed back to the Big House for a night alone.

Back at the Big House, missing Mr P already, I decided to cheer myself up by sending him a photo. Hanging in Mr P's bathroom, there was a picture of a sexy lady posing in front of a fireplace. Most of Mr P's pictures were of birds of prey, but this bird, he said, was one of his favourites. I put on my sexiest underwear and positioned my iPad on the couch in front of the big fire in the drawing-room. I set the ten-second delay timer on the camera and ran to the fireplace, assuming a sexy pose. As usual it took me about ten attempts before I was even in shot, let alone looking sexy. At one point I swear I saw someone at the window but decided I must be imagining it. I eventually chose a photo and sent it to Mr P's phone. It wasn't long before he replied, absolutely delighted with his picture but also mentioning he'd just received a text from his window cleaner rearranging for the following week...

That evening, having closed all the shutters, I busied myself cooking a meal and trying to get the hang of using an Aga. I spent most of my time in the kitchen, I loved that kitchen. Milo took up his position lying in front of the Aga whilst I pottered about. I'd decided, seeing as Mr P was away, to cook baked beans on toast, a change from our usual roast dinner. But could I find a can opener? I had opened every cupboard and drawer but to no avail. But as luck would have it I did come across a large box of Maltesers and settled for them instead.

That night as I lay in bed, alone, I heard the distant chime of the grandfather clock strike his midnight hour. It reminded me of a book I'd read as a child, called the Secret Garden. The story was: there was a little boy living in his Aunt's big old house, and each night, upon hearing the clock strike midnight, he would creep out of his bed and venture into the walled garden, wearing his pyjamas. He would then be taken back in time to the olden days of this big old house and play in the walled garden with the ghost of a little girl. I was so tempted to get out of bed and go to the walled garden. Just to see. It might have been a true story.

The next morning, having not run through the walled garden in my pyjamas, I decided to go and visit my best friend Susan in Perth. I didn't want to be on my own in the Big House, not without Mr P.

My sister Pip and her boyfriend also arranged to drive up to Perth and spend a few days with us in the van.

It was a lovely few days with plenty to catch up on as I told them all about Mr P and all about my travels. As it was a 30-year celebration of the Live Aid concert we had a small party at Susan's house. We all drank copious amounts of alcohol and danced all night. Susan and I did our usual drunken dance on the coffee table which subsequently ended with us both in a heap on the floor. Very late on, I stumbled back to the van to sleep. Pip and her boyfriend had already gone to bed and were fast asleep on the bottom bed when I entered the van. Milo was asleep on the floor, by the door. In my drunken stupor, I stepped over Milo and then tried to climb over the sleeping bodies to reach my ladder. I was quite impressed that I didn't step on any part of their bodies and disturb their sleep. As I put my foot on the first rung of the ladder I felt it wobble slightly, stepping onto the second rung I felt the ladder sway back towards the bed below. I hung on tight, holding my breath and telling myself 'I can do this'. Then as I stepped up to the third rung the ladder swayed right back, held me in mid-air for a moment and then launched me backwards onto the bodies below me. Milo woke up at this point, began barking like a crazy dog and jumping all over us on the bed thinking it was a game.

Chapter 15

It was so lovely to be with friends and family but I was also missing Mr P. He was driving back from London today. It was time to pack up The Beast and hit the road back to the Big house. The road to Mr P's felt good, it felt like I was driving home. Although I once again drove right past his house and had to turn back a few miles down the road, again arriving with the house on my left.

Mr P was back from London and we had guests in the house. This was to become a regular occurrence over the next few months. Lots of Mr P's friends came to stay either for the love of hawking or the hospitable nature of Mr P.

These guests included Richard, an old friend from Cambodia, who was accompanied by his twelve-year old son, Sarrick. Also visiting was big Phil, an old hawking buddy who also happened to be a chef.

Richard wasn't in great health and spent most days sat by the fire in the morning room. Sarrick was quite happy to spend his days throwing a ball for Milo, this pleased me. And big Phil provided a different culinary delight every day, a welcome change from our usual roast dinner.

During our first evening back together Mr P told me about his business in London. It was a strange story. He told me he'd met up with an old flame from years gone by. She was American and was visiting the UK for a few days. He said he felt the need to meet up with her and explain to her why their romance had never blossomed. This he explained, was due to the fact that during their relationship she had cut her long hair short. He said he never quite saw her the same way again and he chose to abruptly end their relationship. But, nearly thirty years later, he felt he owed her an explanation. I'm not quite sure if he told her it was due to her cutting her locks because he said she fell asleep mid conversation. I, at this point, butted in and questioned where he was sleeping? He assured me I had nothing to worry about, they had a twin-bedded room and her hair was still short. I tried to make sense of this conversation, making a mental note to never cut my hair short.

Later in the week we were joined by Mr P's friend, Lily. Ah Missy Lily. Lily was young, attractive and highly vivacious. This was when I began to realise quite what a flirt Mr P was. I initially struggled with the attention he afforded Lily and being a typical female I felt threatened by Lily's presence. I was actually more annoyed by myself, for feeling jealous. But that all changed the day we went hawking.

Neither Lily or I had ever participated in the hawking activity. But we were both keen to add this to our tick list. I was a little apprehensive due to my fear of birds. In fact, I have a fear of any creature with wings. I remember once, being at a garden party in my parents' house when a large bumble bee landed on my skirt. I stood up screaming hysterically, jumping up and down to try and shake it off. Because the bee had latched itself onto my skirt, probably more terrified than me, I chose to rip my skirt off to separate us. I then stopped screaming, looked around, and took in all the open-mouthed stares from my parents and their guests, as I stood there; in just my panties and t-shirt.

Mr P spent most of the morning guiding Miss Lily and I through the do's and don'ts and all that was etiquette out on the moor. We were meeting up with a group of gentlemen friends on the moor. They had all travelled up for a week of hawking and had hired a cottage with a gilly. This was an annual activity for them and they all had their own birds of prey and Pointer dogs in tow. They were quite a well to do bunch of fellas.

Mr P, in his kindness, had provided me with a midge hat. Midges were known to be rife on the moor. I was a little put out by this, as we were all introduced to the gentlemen, Lily looking rather glam, me looking like a bee keepers' assistant. So, I accidentally left the midge hat in Mr P's car.

We all then clambered into various Land Rovers and headed deep into the moors. We had dogs sitting on our laps and Hawks tied up in the back, wearing cute little hats to obscure their vision. The drive was rough, the terrain extremely bumpy and the dogs were pretty excited. Lily and I were in the front land rover accompanied by three, rather dashing young gentlemen. This is when our giggling began.

Once we'd reached what was deemed to be a suitable spot to find the grouse, we parked up the Land Rovers. The dogs excitedly ran off across the moors and we all followed, in search of said grouse. Mr P caught up with me, grabbed hold of my hand and chastised me for forgetting my midge hat. Then there was some activity from the group, the dogs were 'pointing', apparently grouse were in the bracken. There seemed to be a buzz of excitement so I let go of Mr P's hand and ran towards the others. I then caught up with Lily who, it appeared was stuck in a bog. Her wellie boot had sunk into the mud and she couldn't get out. I grabbed both her hands and attempted to pull her out, at the same time losing my footing and falling flat on my backside into another bog. We were both crying with laughter and the more we laughed the more we sank.

Eventually we crawled out of the bog, held hands, and zigzagged through the marsh to re-join the group. This is when I believe the gilly 'flushed' the grouse out and the birds were let off their tethers. Lily and I both exclaimed at the sheer wonderment of seeing the hawk swoop through the sky and witnessing the grouse appear. The occasion didn't provide a catch so we trekked miles further for another try.

Lily had her eye on a particular gentleman in the group and was being her chatty self with him. Mr P disapproved of this behaviour on the moor and told her she needed to keep her voice down. This was serious stuff, we were told, this hawking. Lily and I quietened down at this telling off and both sulked slightly.

After hours of plodding on the moors and not a single grouse in our catch we called it a day and headed back to the cottage. Dogs were fed and watered and birds were caged. We then all gathered in the cottage and I took up residence in front of the gas fire. I was chilled to the bone. Beers and biscuits were handed out and I soon cheered up. That is until I felt a burning sensation on the back of my leg. I'd stood so close to the fire that my leopard print welly had melted into the back of my jeans. I was screaming hysterically and hopping around the room begging someone to rip my welly of. Mr P came to my rescue and removed the melted welly. He then decided it was time to take Lily and me home. Lily peeled herself off her gentleman, I mean couch, and we left.

We were both given a good talking to in the car by Mr P, he said we'd both behaved like children on a school trip, and it was unlikely we'd be invited onto the moors again. I winked at Lily in the car mirror. Miss Lily and I were now best friends.

Back at the Big House Lily and I retired to the drawing room and sat by the fire. We laughed about our day on the moor and both agreed we probably didn't deserve to be invited again. Lily filled me in with the details of her gentleman friend and informed me that all the hawking gentlemen had been invited to Mr P's annual grouse dinner later that week. She was pretty excited about this, and I was excited for her, and not just because it refocused Mr P's attentions back onto me.

Chapter 16

Mr P's annual grouse dinner was, it seemed, very important to him. There were to be about thirty guests from all parts of the world, that being the hawking world. He had prepared a menu for big Phil to cook and we were all provided with our given tasks for the lead up. Richard was more than happy to sit by all the fires and be on fire guard duty all week. Big Phil tried his best to keep on top of Mr P's constant menu changes. Sarrick was still happy to keep Milo entertained with games of catch. Lily and I spent hours planning her forthcoming romance. We did also pitch in to help, attempting to clean and polish the vast amount of crockery, cutlery and crystal glasses.

Mr P spent most of the week mowing the lawns. It seemed that when Mr P was stressed he would jump on the mower and cut the grass, for hours. This activity usually involved Milo chasing the mower and trying to bite the wheels. This added to Mr P's stress.

I had noticed a change in Mr P of late. He was snapping at everybody, me included and was always arguing with our guests. He seemed to have distanced himself from me and chose to go to bed early most nights. I decided that once the falconry dinner was out the way he would calm down again. Unfortunately, his mood was intensifying and big Phil, the chef, got the brunt of it. This caused big Phil to leave the Big House, taking his culinary skills with him. I could now see Mr P going into meltdown, so Lily and I took it upon ourselves to convince him that we could cook this banquet for thirty people. Now I'd never cooked for more than four people and I don't think Lily had ever even cooked. But somehow, we managed to convince Mr P all would be fine. We altered the menu to keep it simple. Mr P would be in charge of the roast meat, we would serve a cold paté starter and Lily suggested a strawberry Pavlova for dessert. Most would be prepared in advance and stored in all of the four fridges Mr P owned. I don't know why he had four fridges, or two washing machines or two dishwashers, he just did.

The day of the dinner arrived and we were all rushing about in preparation. Except Richard, Richard was sat by the fire in the breakfast room. I tried to assist by laying the tables but got quite flustered with the amount of cutlery and glassware, so Mr P took over this task. The meats were in the Aga, slow roasting, the vegetables were prepared and ready to cook. The Pavlova Lily and I had made, or what was left of it, was in the fridge and the paté was plated. We all then headed to our rooms and prepared to dress for dinner.

This was to be the first time Mr P would see me in my glad rags so I made an extra effort on his behalf. When I'd started my adventure I'd packed that one little black dress for, hopefully, a special gentleman. Tonight was that occasion. I checked myself in the mirror and thought I looked pretty damn good for a change. Then I headed downstairs for Mr P's approval. I certainly got his approval. He gave me that approving look he'd given me the first day he met me, I felt good. Unfortunately, that feeling didn't last, Mr P didn't even glance in my direction for the remainder of the entire evening. Once the guests arrived his stress mode kicked in and I seemed to morph into a member of staff. I spent most of the evening in the kitchen or running around at Mr P's requests. He sat at the head of the table lording it all night. Lily was absolutely occupied with her beau and Richard was asleep by the fire in the morning room. The dinner table conversation seemed to be mainly about the grouse season and I felt totally out of my depth. In-between filling the dishwashers and various other tasks I was seemingly knocking back a large amount of fizz. Late in the evening I wandered upstairs to check on Milo and basically passed out in the dog bed with him. I do recall, at some point, hearing Mr P say to someone "and this is my room...oh dear...I do apologise, maybe we should just leave her sleeping..."

The next morning I hauled myself out of the dog basket and went downstairs. Here I found Milo with his head inside the swivel bin eating goodness knows what. The dining room looked like a typical morning-after-the-party scene and the kitchen, my beautiful kitchen, had not fared well either. I started another load in the dishwasher, remembering my instructions not to place the crystal in the dishwasher. The crystal was to be washed by hand, rinsed and then placed on towels, on racks above the Aga. As was the silver cutlery. The stainless steel cutlery was allowed into the dishwasher. With a banging head I knuckled down.

Late in the morning, whilst having coffee with Lily in the drawing room, she informed me of her success with her gentleman friend and their stolen kisses in the walled garden. She also told me that before going to bed she'd had words with Mr P about his lack of attention towards me during the evening. He apparently hadn't realised and had promised to make it up to me.

Later that day, after much lawn mowing, Mr P apologised for his recent behaviour, he admitted he'd been stressed all week and had taken it out on those dearest to him. He then suggested we could organise an afternoon of rifle shooting, to compensate, he explained. I just looked at him.

Guns. Another activity of which neither Lily or I had experience. We were, justly so, rather excited at the prospect. I suggested we blacken our faces with camouflage paint, pop twigs in our hair and go hunt in the woods. Mr P quickly butted in that this was not a game and we must pay attention to all his instructions. Mr P laid a picnic blanket on the lawn. A short row of little silver ducks sat on the garden wall several yards away. We were then given in-depth instructions of the gun's operation and example shots at how and when it was safe to fire at the ducks. I felt a sulk coming on but defused it with my first shot pinging straight into the head of that little silver duck. Lily was right on target too.

The next day Mr P was suited and booted in his plus fours and was preparing to take some French guests up onto the moors for hawking. Lily and I were not invited. We sat in the drawing room, each with our books, and re-christened it the library. After about an hour of our small intimate book club we were both bored. I suggested we wander down to Mr P's boat house on the loch and take the boat out. Lily thought this was an excellent idea. Another unexplored activity to tick off our tick list. Boating. How hard can it be?

We told Mr P of our plan to take the boat out and he hesitantly agreed it would be OK. He did advise us that no one had been down to the boat house in well over a year and it could be in a state of disrepair. This didn't put us off. Before he left for the moor he drew us a small map of the path we should to take down to the loch.

Lily and I prepared ourselves for our adventure. We wore hats, gloves, wellies and sunglasses as were the all-important life jackets Mr P insisted we wear. I took a photo of the map on my phone and stuffed it into my coat pocket with a decent supply of chocolate bars. And off we went.

Our first mistake was not reading the map. We found ourselves not on a footpath but in a large boggy field full of some pretty angry looking sheep and clusters of large prickly thistles. Parts of the field were dotted with quite deep streams and as Lily's wellies were only ankle height we had to jump them or avoid them. Lily discovered she wasn't very good at jumping and ended up with wellies full of water.

We could see the little red boathouse in the distance and took a route following the barbed wire fence along the field. When we reached the boathouse we found it was gated and locked with a very rusty looking padlock. We therefore had to launch ourselves over the gate, I think that's when I lost my chocolate bars.

The boathouse did look a bit neglected, the paint was peeling and the weeds around it were waist high. But we managed to pull back the large double doors and there she was. The boat. Now I'm not very clued up on boats, in fact I've never sailed in a boat, but this boat didn't look healthy to me. I don't know if we were expecting to find a luxury, motor driven yacht equipped with all the mod cons and a dashing young pilot at the helm, but this was not what we found. It was basically just a wooden tub and pretty rotten looking wood at that. We eyed up the boat and judged the distance to the shore of the loch. At that moment we made the decision that the boat wouldn't even make it to the shore let alone float on the water.

So we just sat in the boat, in the boathouse, an oar each in hand and rocked side to side. That's when we discovered we'd lost the chocolate.

On our venture back to the Big House we chose to avoid the boggy field and cross a flatter looking field. This was fine until we spotted some pretty large cows meandering towards us. We hastily threw ourselves over the barbed wire fence back into the boggy field and rejoined the angry sheep. They seemed less threatening than the cows. Back at the Big House Richard asked us how we'd got on with the boat, we both admitted our sailing days were over before they'd begun.

Mr P was still out hawking so Lily and I returned to our book club, with a nice well-earned bottle of red. I went off to the downstairs bathroom and whilst washing my hands I marvelled to myself at how many coats and hats Mr P had hanging on the rails. I began trying on the hats, posing in the big mirror. When I returned to the drawing room Lily glanced up from her book and just burst into a fit of giggles. I was wearing a very large and very long waxed coat with Mr P's oversized gumboots. I had on my head a deer stalking hat and was carrying a very ornate deer stalking stick. I looked ridiculous, like some kind of Sherlock Holmes wannabe. Lily excitedly jumped up and insisted I find her some similar attire. We headed back to the bathroom and Lily dressed in a costume even more ridiculous than mine. We then both bounced into the morning room to give Richard and Sarrick a fashion show. They both agreed we looked both sensational and ridiculous and couldn't stop laughing. Then we all headed to the garden and had our photos taken under the flagpole.

Minutes later, we heard a car coming up the drive and bolted back into the house before Mr P saw us. Our main fear being he had brought the French guests back to introduce us to. Mind you we could have probably got away with pretending this was normal attire when living at the Big House.

The following day I woke up with a sadness. My Miss Lily was returning south. Her visit was over all too soon. I thought of how threatened I'd felt when she first arrived at The Big House and now I felt like I was losing my best friend, my little partner in crime. Mr P and I drove her to Inverness airport and waved her off in the terminal. I told Mr P it was like waving off the daughter I'd never had, like she was leaving us and heading off to university.

"When will we see her again?" I cried, "I miss her so much already."

"Do you think she'll phone, maybe I should call her tonight." I continued

"Don't worry darling, I'll cheer you up. Let me take you shopping." Mr P enthused.

Inverness was the first big city I'd shopped in for what felt like forever. I was quite excited. Mr P suggested we purchase some underwear for me, I readily agreed. I spent forever choosing, undecided on style or colour and continually asking Mr P's approval. Eventually we agreed on a classy black and gold selection and headed to the counter to pay. Then

Mr P asked me if I'd brought the vouchers Susan had given me for my birthday? I duly handed them over. I had wondered why he'd chosen to take me to Marks & Spencer for my sexy underwear.

After wandering around all the tobacco shops to replenish his electric pipe fluid we headed back to the Big House.

That evening Mr P decided as the weather was turning a bit chilly we would move bedrooms. We would now sleep in the maids room above the kitchen. What with our thousand thread sheets, pure goose down duvet, tapestry throws and the heat of the Aga rising through the floorboards, I felt like I was sleeping in the Bahamas. It was a restless night.

Chapter 17

Life had quietened down somewhat since Lily had left so I threw myself into domestic bliss. I took up baking. I found some Aga cook books, a tartan pinny and began with the cake section. Mr P loved my cookies but my scones were a bit more like rock cakes and my pancakes were stodgy. I stuck to the cookies and baked them nearly every day. I'd found a swanky bicycle in the big shed and had taken to riding round the garden every day, looking for Mr P with my cookies in hand. I'd also found the most amazing, unused, electric iron in the big shed. It was like ironing butter and I took it upon myself to iron all Mr P's posh shirts. Then I got to work on the garden. I started with all the dead leaves at the main gate. I was fed up slushing through them every day when we drove in and out. I had asked Mr P why he didn't have an electric gate and his response was he'd not get to witness the wiggle of my cute backside if I didn't have to open the gate. I granted him that.

After a time domestic bliss was wearing me down. Not that I'm lazy but I felt I was becoming a Stepford wife. So, I decided I would find myself a job. This would also give me an income to chip in paying my way. Because, for all the grandeur we were living in, I was well aware that Mr P was not a rich man. Trouble was there weren't many jobs available in the Caithness area. I was so used to seeing vacancies arise on jobs sites hourly at least. Here, it averaged a few new vacancies per week.

So I took the initiative, jumped in The Beast and headed down to the local bar and restaurant. I ordered a coffee and sat in the lounge area surveying the establishment. The average age of the staff was about eighteen. Yes, I would fit in nicely here, I thought. When I left to pay I stopped at the reception desk and enquired with the manager of any staff vacancies. I was informed there was nothing just now but they took my details anyway. Unfortunately, when I left the manager was watching me at the door, he saw me get into The Beast, Milo's head hanging out the window, and no doubt thought I was some sort of traveller, I never heard back from him.

Life floated along for Mr P and me. Milo seemed pretty settled too. One of his favourite activities was chasing the rabbits around the grounds. Sadly most of them had myxomatosis and were therefore blind, they would just run round in circles until they hit a tree. Then Milo would just bark at them because they had stopped running, sometimes they would stand on their back legs and try to box him, this confused Milo. One of mine and Mr P's favourite activities was watching the rooks. Most evenings around dusk he would call me to the garage. I would sit on the couch with him and he would flick the electric garage door open. Then we would first hear them and then see them approaching the Big House in the sky.

They were heading for the big trees to settle for the evening, hundreds and hundreds of them, filling the sky and turning it black. Even though I was terrified of birds I felt safe watching them with Mr P. It usually took about ten minutes before the sky cleared and their squawking quietened. I loved this spectacle. Mr P hated the mess they left on the ground though.

My mornings were spent walking with Milo on the brae and my afternoons pottering around the house. In a big house there is always work to be done and given the fact that I love cleaning I was in my element. Although I did regret deciding to clean the inside windows, it took me most of one day just to clean one, the sheer size of them involved the use of a tall ladder. Most days we'd pop into town to do food shopping, whereupon Mr P always insisted on pushing the trolley and choosing the food which invariably consisted of roast meat, new potatoes and leeks. One day I suggested we have spicy chicken and baked potato with coleslaw. Mr P reluctantly went along with this.

"That was so tasty wasn't it?" I said observing his clean plate

"It was fine, Nicci, but I wouldn't eat it again." he replied politely

It was back to new boiled potatoes after that.

One evening I persuaded Mr P to turn on the television. We never really watched TV, and this didn't bother me, but tonight there was a program on called Who Do You Think You Are? featuring Paul Hollywood. I wanted to watch it, not to see Paul Hollywood, though he is a rather handsome specimen, but because of my sister, Pip.

A few years earlier Pip had fallen down a stone staircase in Chester town centre. When I reached her, she was lying at the bottom unconscious and lifeless. I truly thought she was dead and whilst waiting for the ambulance I held her hand and willed her to open her eyes. She did regain consciousness, was taken to hospital and kept in overnight. Due to her previous brain haemorrhage she underwent various tests and was then declared fit to go home.

Over the coming weeks Pip felt restless and one day picked up a pencil and started doodling. What she drew was amazing, she could copy any picture you placed in front of her be it a dog, cat, person or the like. Her drawings were often better than the photograph she was copying. Over the years she drew most days and when a local art fair in Hoylake came up she decided to go along. Hundreds of local artists displayed their work along the promenade to be admired by the crowds.

As Pip and I sat behind her table displaying a selection of her latest sketches, a lady approached us. She was admiring Pips talent and then exclaimed, "That's my son, Paul." It was Paul Hollywood's mum. She was so impressed with the drawing she asked if she could buy it. Pip was so pleased with this accolade she gave the drawing to her.

And now, as Mr P and I watched the TV, we saw Paul Hollywood walk into his mum's house and there, on the wall, was the drawing Pip had done. Paul even stopped at the drawing and posed next to it saying, "see the likeness?" I was more than proud of Pip that night.

Mr P and I would often sit together on the couch in the garage, drinking milky coffees, admiring his lawns and me listening to his stories. I had figured out, quite early on, that I rarely got to talk about me, but this didn't really bother me. I can pour my soul out when I'm writing but when it comes to actually 'talking' about myself I'm like a closed book. Mr P was so kind and caring and appeared to enjoy being with me, as did I him. He told me, on a daily basis, how happy he was now, with me in his life. He had big plans for our future together in the Big House. He told me we were going to have our happy ever after.

Chapter 18

Eventually we got to a point when we had no guests in the house. Just the two of us. During this period the newspaper that had run my original story contacted me. They were keen to do a follow up story of me meeting my perfect man. They asked if they could send a photographer to the house for pictures of us. Mr P was not at all keen on this idea, he didn't want his picture in the paper. I respected his decision and the newspaper seemed happy to run the story without revealing his identity. The story was printed that weekend and we bought numerous copies of it. Ben, the journalist, wrote a lovely article which in turn produced some lovely feedback on my blog. Mr P was pleased for me.

Within days of this article being printed I was approached by a national newspaper asking if they could interview us for a feature article. They had intentions of flying their journalist and photographer up to The Big House with a wardrobe and make-up technician. They also asked if Mr P would be willing to be in the press. I told them, under no circumstances, would he allow this and I respected his wishes. They then asked if he would be happy to speak on the phone. I passed the phone to Mr P. I didn't hear the conversation, it went on for about an hour. As much as I tried to listen behind closed doors Mr P kept moving around the house. When he eventually got off the phone he informed me we were both going to be in the article. I asked him how they had convinced him to do this and he just said he felt comfortable with them, they seemed professional and had promised to be discreet.

Just before the interview another national newspaper called me asking for our story. I told them I'd already promised it to another paper. They got a bit awkward and said they were running the story anyway with or without my input. I informed the initial paper of this information, so they decided to bring the story forward a few days. This meant we both told our side of the story, to the journalist, over the telephone and a local photographer would be sent to the house tomorrow, without a make-up or wardrobe technician.

They asked me to wear some 'country house' type clothing and I explained, as I'd been travelling in my motor-home my main wardrobe consisted of jeans and hoodies. They said they would reimburse me for any out of pocket expenses. Sadly, this was late in the day and the shops were now closed. So it was a last minute dash to our neighbours house and she kindly let me raid her wardrobe.

The next morning, Mr P seemed quite excited. He'd even found a little tartan collar for Milo to wear. He lit all the fires and repositioned some of the furniture to suit the ambience. He chose to change the flagpole and raised the Falconry flag. I thought it would be quite funny to secretly swap the flag for a pair of his underpants. I didn't do this. He obviously mowed all the lawns before the photographer arrived and then dressed accordingly in his kilt attire looking rather dashing.

I managed to wash and blow dry my hair and apply some make-up without any paid help. Then I threw on my country house outfit.

As we checked ourselves in the mirror I suggested getting a Biro and covering him in tattoos, then we could be photographed as the Posh and Becks of Caithness. Mr P said no.

Although Mr P felt awkward having his picture taken the photographer put him at ease. We had a lovely day and even got to see some of the photographs, of which Mr P approved.

The day of the newspaper publication I got up very early. We hadn't decided who would go to the newsagent to purchase the paper and had discussed wearing a disguise and potentially spending the next month having our groceries delivered. But I didn't even need to leave the house. It was in the on-line edition. And it was the main headline news. I'd never heard anything so crazy in my whole life. Me and Mr P headline news in a national newspaper because we were having a romance. It all seemed so silly reading the headline quoting him as being a Laird and me as Lady of the manor. It felt surreal. Like reading about someone else. We weren't famous, we hadn't done anything extraordinary, it was just our relationship.

But there it was, full colour, full spread, full story. Plus the comments. Why oh why did I read the comments? Big mistake on my part, but once you start you can't stop. They'd already hit over a thousand which is what intrigued me.

Mr P came out rather well in the comments, he seemed to draw some sympathy. I on the other hand fared less well.

They read along the lines of 'hope he did a pre-nup', 'she's a gold digger', 'she must have slept with most of Scotland', 'is that a camper-van or a mattress on her back', 'she looks more like approaching 70 not 50', 'poor guy, she's after his money', etc.

They were written incognito, never a real name attached unless it was a positive comment.

And thankfully there were plenty of positives too. 'Good luck to them', 'nice to read a happy story', 'what a lovely romance'.

This article was, like previously, reprinted all round the world. I still to this day don't know all the publications. It sent my blog viewing figures into overload, to the point of my blog qualifying for advertising space. This impressed me much. Although to date I've made a total amount of about £38. I've still never figured out the analytics of it all but it seems you make about a penny per thousand views. Not so impressive after all.

The house phone in the Big House was constantly ringing for Mr P, he was quite delighted. He joked about who would play him when Hollywood made the movie. Mr P was on an up. He even suggested we had a steak pie from the renowned Bews butchers for our supper, still served with new potatoes though.

Chapter 19

The ink on the newspaper was hardly dry before I received a call from the TV show, This Morning. They wanted to fly Mr P and me down to London to sit on the couch and be interviewed by Holly and Philip. Oh my, I loved Philip Schofield. Sadly this invitation didn't include Milo. Mr P doesn't watch much TV so had never heard of this show. He wasn't too keen to begin with but after various conversations with many of his friends and discovering Sue Ellen of Dallas was also scheduled onto the show he decided we should do it. He saw it as an opportunity to promote the Big House as a wedding venue idea he had and took it as a good business move. I was just excited to be flying to London and staying in a fancy hotel with Mr P.

Two days before our trip to London Mr P's good friend Greg arrived to stay. He was the cutest little man I'd ever met and was the spitting image of the character Norris from Coronation Street, something he had been told often. The night before our flight to London, Norris, as I now called him, and I sat on Mr P's bed whilst Mr P tried on various outfits suitable for a TV appearance. Three different pairs of beige moleskin trousers were tried on, which I thought all looked the same, but Mr P insisted they were quite different. A selection of Blazers, shirts and even different belts were put on taken off and tried again. This fashion show went on for most of the night with Mr P eventually settling for an outfit he felt most comfortable in. I then went to my wardrobe and found a clean pair of black trousers, a smart blouse and my only jacket and chucked them in an overnight bag.

The next morning, we were ready to go. We drove to Inverness airport, stopping for petrol on the way. Mr P insisted I pay as I would be able to claim back the travel expenses from the TV company. This exercise continued on our trip, even down to cups of coffees, I just hoped my credit card would cope.

At Inverness airport I had put my bag through the X-ray machine and was walking away towards the departure lounge. I heard a commotion behind me and looked back to see Mr P standing there with my sexy, black lace bra in his hand with a look of horror on his face. I had apparently wheeled my bag away without zipping it closed and my bra had fallen out. Unfortunately it had landed at Mr P's feet and was picked up by a random stranger who assumed it had come from Mr P's bag. I couldn't stop laughing at this sight, Mr P eventually saw the funny side.

When we arrived at Gatwick airport we were met by a private chauffeur and driven into the city. Our hotel was on the banks of the river Thames and our room had a view of the London Eye. We were greeted at hotel reception with a glass of complimentary champagne, Mr P refused his, I gladly took both. A table had been reserved in the restaurant for our evening meal so we freshened up and headed down. Unfortunately the nearest item to a roast dinner was suckling pig, this tiny portion of pig was served on a large plate with one small potato. And that was it.

For some strange reason Mr P decided to phone an ex-girlfriend during dinner. He proceeded to take his call to a private lounge area beside the restaurant and left me at the table. I found this behaviour a bit odd but took the opportunity to wander out of the hotel in search of some late night snacks. I lost my bearings slightly and was wandering around the streets of London, crisps and chocolate under my arms, looking for the hotel. I did, for a moment, feel quite vulnerable and wondered if I might get mugged, murdered and thrown into a wheelie bin. Mr P probably assuming I was still sitting at the dinner table finishing off his glass of wine. I then gave myself a little talking to, reminding myself I had driven the coast of Scotland, alone, in a van, staying with various strangers and sleeping on cliffs. Nobody was going to steal my chocolate.

Back at the hotel Mr P was still deep in conversation so I headed back to our room, stuffed my face and fell asleep.

The next morning we headed down for breakfast. The choice was immense, even for some reason a tray of peas were on offer. I hate peas. Peas frighten me.

We were both quite nervous about our day ahead so ate very little. I just drank copious amounts of coffee.

Back in our room reception called to inform us our chauffeur was here to collect us. The chauffeur drove us to the TV studio, which was literally about a two minute walk away. We were greeted at the door by an official looking security guard and taken to the Green Room.

Wow, me in a Green Room. And it actually was painted a subtle green colour. There were pastries laid on the table and pots of hot fresh coffee. On the wall was a huge TV screen blaring out the station we were to appear on. We were the first guests to arrive and were soon taken into make-up. Mr P was most uncomfortable with this. We were both sat in make-up chairs in front of a large brightly lit mirror and assigned a make-up artist each. I could see Mr P, out the corner of my eye, squirming in his seat as they tried to apply foundation on his face. I was lapping it up, I'd never had this before and was savouring every moment. The girl applying my make-up thought ours was a wonderful story, she even asked me for a list of my rejects, she being single. I was most impressed at how the girl hid the dark shadows under my eyes. I wasn't too enamoured with my hair and made a discreet visit to the ladies to buff it up a bit.

Back in the Green Room, Mr P was happily chatting with two other guests. They were brothers and ran a successful gardening company in

London. Mr P was in his element telling them all about his garden and plans he had for it. It didn't take long for his mood to drop though, as I had to inform him that Sue Ellen would not be joining us as hers was to be a satellite interview. I thought telling him that the Osmond brothers were on the show might cheer him up. It didn't.

I was most interested in the next guest to join us in the Green Room. Tracey Cox was a sex therapist. I wanted to ask her so many questions but held back so as not to embarrass myself or Mr P.

Before our turn came to sit on the couch with Philip and Holly we went outside so Mr P could smoke his electric pipe. Whilst outside we met Rylan Clark from the show. He was so friendly and chatted away to us about how lovely our story was. When he'd left I said to Mr P how excited I was to have met Rylan. Mr P did not know who Rylan was and thought we'd been chatting to a member of the production team.

The show was now live and we were sat waiting for our call to go on. For once I was so glad to have Mr P hold my hand, I was so nervous. Then they called us to the studio. We walked in behind the cameras and could see the big red couch ahead. Philip and Holly were saying goodbye to their previous guest and the make-up artist was trying to add a little touch up make-up onto my face. At that moment the production manager said, "We don't have time for that." and I questioned what on earth he meant by that remark. He just laughed and said "Right, you're on." and pushed us towards the couch.

And there we were. Sitting on the big red couch beside Philip and Holly on live TV. I was aware of a whole production crew in front of me but was quite blinded by all the lights. As soon as Holly and Philip said hello I quite forgot where I was and just started chatting like I was with friends. They were so lovely to both of us it honestly didn't feel like live TV. It was all over so quickly and I turned to Mr P to ask if he was OK, he looked uncomfortable so I gave him a little kiss and squeezed his hand. What I didn't realise was the cameras were still rolling and this scene was being broadcast on live TV. Philip and Holly thought this was so sweet.

On the way back to the Green room we passed some elderly people in the corridor. I thought they were maybe next in line to be interviewed and wondered what their story was. Back in the Green room I saw them on the live screen being introduced as the Osmonds.

All too soon it was time for us to leave the studio and our chauffeur had arrived to drop us anywhere we liked in the city. Driving out of the studio gates I spotted a crowd of people waiting for a glimpse of a celebrity. I had to do it. I wound down my window and waved at the crowd. I did hear someone say 'who's that' to which someone replied 'oh that's the girl who travelled to Scotland and met a Lord.' Yeay! I grinned to myself, I'm a celebrity, today. We chose to be dropped at the nearest café whereupon I took out my iPad and tried to live stream the interview. I was so excited but Mr P did not want to watch it and I believe still hasn't to this day.

Me with the lovely Phillip Schofield...

We arrived at Gatwick airport far too early for our flight back to Inverness. So we had a few hours to kill wandering round the airport. We ended up sitting in a café where a lady approached our table and exclaimed how she had watched us on TV that morning. I thought this was so funny and wondered about buying a large hat and shades for the rest of our journey. Mr P said I was overreacting and should calm down. The rest of our journey home was quite boring.

We got back to the Big House late into the night. Mr P had taken a phone call so handed me the door keys. I ran into the house and was greeted by a very excited Milo. I'd only been gone one night but had missed him like crazy. Mr P took ages on the phone and then appeared at the kitchen window. I'd apparently locked the door behind me and he couldn't get in the house. The actual truth, I subsequently found out, was Mr P was talking to his girlfriend. Well, she had believed she was his girlfriend until she'd switched on the TV that morning and seen us both on the couch with Philip and Holly. As far as she was aware she was in a relationship with Mr P and was completely unaware of my existence. Wow! what a way to be dumped, on live TV. In time to come I was to find out that, according to Mr P, she was a casual fling who he rarely saw and had ended this supposed relationship before I arrived in his life. Breakdown in communication is what I thought to myself. Or someone is lying?

There appeared to be cracks forming in our relationship. Something wasn't quite right. In such a short space of time I'd declared my wonderful romance with Mr P to a worldwide audience. And yet I felt like I was sharing him with various other females. And that's not to mention the private and constant contact with his ex-wife.

I'd recently answered the house phone when Mr P was out hawking. A lady had enquired as to who I was and upon my reply she said "Oh, so you're the supposed air hostess." she continued without a pause, "well you tell Mr P I called and, as I well know, on his return from the moors he does like to immediately take a shower, so I will expect his call after supper."

Well, that was me told. Mr P found this quite amusing and pestered me all night for the whole conversation. And, duly called her back after supper. Behind a closed door.

Chapter 20

I wasn't feeling great but was cheered up with the knowledge my best friend, Sue was coming to stay for the weekend. I was so looking forward to her visit.

The day before Sue arrived I was sitting on the couch in the garage watching Mr P mow the lawns when I received a voice-mail. It was from one of the radio stations asking if they could do a catch-up interview. I called them right back and was put on hold whilst waiting to speak to the presenter. Whilst I was on hold Milo decided to do his mad dog impression and chase Mr P who was sat on the lawn mower. I could see Mr P trying to shake Milo's teeth from his trouser leg and getting quite annoyed with him. I ran onto the lawn screaming at Milo and trying to distract him with a ball. Milo let go of Mr P's ankle but then chose to try and bite the tyres. I carried on running across the lawn, yelling at him, leave. What I didn't realise, until I heard a little voice in my ear piece, was I had been transferred through to the presenter on the phone and was being recorded for the interview. Luckily it was pre-recorded and they were able to edit my screaming fit before airing.

Later that day two more guests arrived to stay at the Big House. The husband brought with him a grand selection of guns and camera equipment, the wife brought oxygen tanks. The wife was rather unwell and was hoping for a quiet vacation. The husband was hoping to capture some wildlife. That evening we all sat in the dining room for a roast dinner, Mr P had lit the big fire. Unfortunately there was some sort of blockage in the chimney breast and when the wife retired to bed, her room, above the dining room, was filled with smoke. Knowing she relied on oxygen tanks we offered her another room but she chose to sleep with the windows open instead. There was a chill throughout the whole house that night.

The next day the husband went off to explore the garden to set up his night vision time delay cameras to capture some action. I wandered around the walled garden with the wife. She took this opportunity to question my intentions regarding Mr P. She asked me if I thought he was enjoying being in the media and did I request his permission to write about him in my blog. I told her that Mr P made his own decisions regarding the media and he was well aware of the content of my blog. I got the feeling she didn't like me very much but as she was a friend of Mr P's I shook it off.

That evening Sue was due to arrive and I was waiting at the end of the drive with a torch. I was like a kid on Christmas Eve and was terrified she would drive past the house, as I usually did, and end up lost in the dark. I was so excited about her arrival, as I'd said to Mr P, she was the first guest I would not have to be introduced to. I'd warned Mr P that Sue and I would chatter away like teenagers all weekend and he said he just wanted Sue to feel at home in our home. That felt nice. Our home.

When I saw her car approaching I flashed the torch light beckoning her into the drive. I closed the gate behind her and jumped into her car. There were squeals of hysteria and hugs abundant. We thought it best to get this display of crazy girlfriend reunions out the way before going into the house. Whilst in the car I warned Sue about the tense atmosphere with the other guests and she had the bright idea of hunting out the night vision cameras and glaring into the lens like something out a horror movie. I thought this was a fabulous idea so we made a plan to sneak out when everyone went to bed.

I took Sue through the garage and into the kitchen, she loved the kitchen nearly as much as me. Milo was most excited to see her, like me, he needed no introduction. I then took her through to the drawing room to meet Mr P and our other guests. Sue is ever so pretty and this didn't go unnoticed by Mr P. Or our other male guest. Sue pulled out a bottle of wine from her handbag at which point our guests chose to retire to bed. Mr P sat with us for a while until he got bored of our girl talk and left us to it. But not before he kindly supplied us with a big bag of chocolate buttons. Sue and I drank so much wine we completely forgot about our plan to hijack the garden cameras and tried to quietly tiptoe to bed. In-between all our hush hushes and banging into walls I don't think we were quiet at all. When I crept into our room Mr P was not in our bed, it baffled me for a moment until I remembered we had moved rooms again. Sleeping above the Aga had proved to be too hot and we'd returned to the main house bedroom. I snook in next to him and he didn't murmur.

The next morning Sue said she'd slept well although she told Mr P she was most disappointed at the lack of a chocolate mint on her pillow. We both sat in the kitchen, sharing the stool, and drank pots and pots of coffee. Then we took a wander into the town for more coffee.

Back at the Big House we found Mr P mowing the lawns and the other guests had gone off exploring. I took Sue into the big shed, which she decided was more like an aircraft hangar, to show her my bicycle. We amused ourselves for a while with the table tennis and darts, which neither of us were very good at. Then Sue found a gorgeous horse saddle on a stand and a leather lasso. I don't know why Mr P had this equipment as there was no horse. This didn't stop us from acting out a rodeo display in the shed. With all the noise we were making Mr P appeared in the doorway, he just grinned at us and could see we were having fun. He then asked if we'd like to take the quad bike out on the brae. I'd never been allowed to drive the quad bike so was eager to accept. After our instructions were given and repeated back off we went. We felt like Hells Angels roaring up and down the driveway. We took the roundabout at such speed we accidentally sprayed gravel all over the car bonnet of our returning guests. The quad bike was grudgingly returned to the shed.

I think the gentleman guest could see we were looking for some fun. He suggested we get the guns set up and go do some target practice. Sue and I were definitely up for this. His wife chose to go for a lie down.

These were big guns so we paid extra attention to our instructions. We were positioned on the table above the walled garden and our target was on a tree across the lake on the brae. We couldn't see the target until we looked down the barrel of the gun. And even though I'd been warned about the kick back I'd feel on my shoulder it still came as a shock when I pulled the trigger. I felt like a true marksman firing at that tree. I'm pretty sure I was way off target but was informed I did really well.

That evening we all sat in the dining room for another roast dinner. Sue sat next to our gentleman guest and having downed a few glasses of red, told him of our plan to hijack his cameras. He thought this was hysterical. We all had quite a laugh round the dinner table that night, well most of us did. Our gentleman guest suggested we finish our bottle of wine in the drawing room by the fire. Once Sue and I had cleared the table we bounced through to join the party. Our gentleman guest then informed us he was no longer drinking and he and his wife were going to bed. She didn't say a word. I think there had been words already.

The following day, Sue had to return to Perth. I was feeling quite distraught. There was an atmosphere in the house I didn't much like. Sue gave me her usual blubbering goodbye, Sue cries at the drop of a hat. I, who very rarely cries, found myself shedding a little tear on her departure. I waved her off down the road and then trudged up the drive back to the Big House. Milo was sitting in the doorway of the van with a tennis ball in his mouth. He looked sad too.

I sat with Milo in The Beast listening to my favourite CD, LA Freeway. After about an hour there was a tap on the door, it was Mr P. He asked if he could come in. He said he needed to talk to me.

Mr P sat beside me on my couch, he didn't take my hand like he normally did. He seemed flustered and made some small talk about how quaint it was inside my van. In all the time I'd been with Mr P this was his first venture to the inside of my van.

He then told me that with much thought and deliberation he wanted me to stop writing my blog. He also said he wanted me to remove every blog entry I had written since meeting him. I was dumbfounded. I questioned what had brought him to this decision. He tried to explain he didn't feel comfortable with it anymore and he didn't like what I had written about him. I asked him which bit he didn't like and he struggled to give me an example. All he could come up with was when I'd written that he looked like the honey monster when he woke in the morning. I found that quite lame especially as it had been written as a term of endearment. I tried to argue that this was who I am, that he had met me through my blog, it had brought us together. I told him I loved writing my blog, I was always discreet in what I published, and it was a part of my life. He was having none of it and basically let it be known he was not backing down on his decision. I questioned if it really was his decision or had he been influenced by somebody else over the weekend. He did admit that a certain someone had thought my blog was not good for our relationship.

I sat in my van for a while, once he'd gone back into the house, thinking about what felt like an ultimatum. Mr P had always enthused about my blog, he'd seemed quite proud of my writing. He'd provided me with my own little writing area in his study and actively encouraged me to write. I was well aware that he'd led a somewhat quiet life before I'd arrived but I was also aware of how he told me, on a regular basis, how happy I'd made him feel. How I'd awakened him and given him purpose. He loved my spirit and enthusiasm, days in the Big House were so much better with Milo and me there.

Now it felt like he was crushing all of that. Now he wanted to change all of that. Now I felt like he was removing a part of me.

As much as what Mr P had asked of me had hurt me, I chose to go along with his request. I said if it really bothered him so much then I would stop writing. I would stop writing for him. I wanted our relationship to work and if that meant compromise then so be it. Unfortunately it didn't feel like a compromise.

The next morning I was up early and walking Milo on the brae. I looked over to the Big House and could see our guests packing their car. By the time I got back to the house I saw their car going out the gate. They'd decided to leave two days early and chose to make their escape whilst I was out. Not even a goodbye. Huh. I was glad to see them go.

Chapter 21

Over the next few days Mr P mowed the lawns. A lot. Every time I looked out the window I could see him, through his clouds of pipe smoke, driving up and down on the mower. He had such a sadness in his eyes. He'd stopped telling me all his stories, which I actually found myself missing. He'd taken to going for long drives, alone, to 'think'. He'd spend hours on the phone, behind closed doors, talking to goodness knows who. He seemed to be avoiding my company in the Big House, rarely talking to me, only to occasionally snap at me or put me down. He went to bed very early most nights and would wake at the crack of dawn. My morning milky coffees and hugs had stopped. Whenever I entered a room he'd exit. It was all becoming quite unbearable. One of us had to do something to change this. And I realised this would have to be me.

After what had felt like the longest and loneliest week of my life I asked Mr P if we could sit down and talk.

"Are you happy?" I tentatively asked him

He took my hands in his and looked deep into my eyes

"Are you happy, Darling?" he replied

I think at this point we had realised that neither of us were happy. Mr P went on to say he had asked me to change, to become someone I was not. He'd crushed my spirit, the one thing that had excited him to have me in his life, he had removed. He hated himself for this and was so very sorry. But he couldn't change. He couldn't keep up with my love of life, my sense of adventure, my passion to explore. He didn't want to hold me back from all things wonderful but felt he could not make me happy. He said he so desperately wanted me as a part of his life but feared he'd never be enough for me.

The summer was over and the long nights were drawing in. Money was tight and job prospects were low. Mr P was sinking into a sadness that I was unable to draw him out of. We were from different worlds Mr P and I. I wanted us to move on and up. Mr P wanted us to stand still. I knew I couldn't make him happy nor him me. I was pushing him over the edge and I couldn't be held responsible for that. I made a decision. I decided I had to leave Mr P. I knew it would break his heart if I left but I also knew the pain I was putting him through by staying.

Mr P cried. He cried like I'd never seen a man cry before. Then he lay his head in my lap and I stroked his head as he sobbed. He told me I was right to leave and he had not a single regret of what we'd had together. He said he never had, and probably never would again, met anyone quite like me. I was the only person in his life who had managed to lift his spirit, even for just a moment. And he thanked me for this. He said I was the stronger person and he admired my courage in making this decision for us. We were both so sad but knew our fairy tale had finished. We'd had one hundred and twenty one days...

I picked a time when Mr P was out to pack my van. To be honest I had very few belongings in the Big House. A small selection of clothes, a few toiletries and Milo's bed. Had I ever belonged here I wondered?

Scanning the bedroom I picked up a pillow from the bed. I tucked it under my arm and walked out. I'm not sure if I took it because it smelt of Mr P or because it was an extremely comfy, soft cotton, John Lewis pillow. Probably the latter.

On our last evening together Mr P cooked me a wonderful meal of poussin and of course boiled potatoes. We shared a decent bottle of wine and sat on the couch together by the fire in the snug. Mr P held me in his arms for what felt like forever and there we made love. For the last time.

There was a sadness in the air in the morning. The whole house seemed down in mood. Neither of us knew what to say to each other so said nothing. After breakfast I decided it was time to leave. I checked I had everything in the van and then went to find Mr P. He was mowing the lawns. I told him I was ready to leave and he said he would walk down to open the gate for me. It was like a scene from a funeral procession. Mr P walking down the long driveway so slowly with his head hung low and me chugging behind him in The Beast.

I wound my window down at the gate and Mr P came towards me. We both had tears in our eyes and an overwhelming sadness in our hearts.

"Take care, my sweetheart." he said, "I will never forget all that you have given me, Darling."

"No regrets, Mr P?" I asked

"No regrets, Nicci." he replied

And off I went.

Half a mile down the road I stopped at his neighbours house. I asked them if they may keep an eye on Mr P. To just look in on him now and again, make sure he was OK. I was genuinely worried for his well-being. Even though our fairy tale was over I still cared deeply for him. Mr P wore his heart on his sleeve, his feelings were soft and vulnerable. Whereas I was strong and tough, my feelings would be buried deep inside.

Extracts from my blog miloandme6.blogspot.com

Maltesers and dead bunnies - 18th August

It's been a busy weekend getting the big house ready for guests next week. Mr P is hosting his annual Falconry Dinner and various people are staying over. I have spent many hours up a ladder cleaning, I've lost count of how many, windows. And these are very old windows with big wooden shutters so you can imagine the dust.

This morning I took Milo round the big field and on the way back found two more dead rabbits. We have an abundance of them here, but they have been hit with myxomatosis . Milo loves to chase them but if he ever catches up with them he does not know what to do with them. Yesterday one of them was boxing him through a fence, so cute.

I then drove Mr P to the airport for a business trip and came back an empty house.   Tried to find a tin opener for my baked beans but to no avail, but did find a box of Maltesers so happy days! Then looking for shampoo I found six bottles of all the same flavour Alberto balsam and one volumising bottle. Lesson learnt, people with thick hair shouldn't choose volumising shampoo. Big hair day.

Good friends and catchups - 22nd August

Saturday morning now and I got my Pip and her boyfriend as guests in my van, tight squeeze but good fun. We went to visit our good friend Sonya from our airhostess days last night in Elie. Was lovely to reminisce about our flying days and the antics we used to get up to.

How we got away with stuff back then! We were waited on hand and foot by husband Olav and daughter Maria, was a perfect evening.

Today we are off to Perth to visit my bestie friend Sue for another catch up and no doubt lots of wine. We are celebrating Live Aid which was actually 30 years ago! Yikes I feel old. I was even living in Wembley then and could hear it all from my flat window. We are going to be hearing all those tunes today and mixed with the alcohol it could get messy!

It's so lovely having guests in my van, I even got to paint my toe nails while they entertained Milo. It does feel a little strange being back in the van since moving into The Big House, but was lovely driving around like a trucker again! I am returning to The Big House on Monday and have a busy week ahead with various guests and entertaining.

Back to the Big House Milo - 25th August

So I'm back in the big house and we have lovely visitors. One gentleman being the most amazing chef, another gentleman full of crazy fun stories and a young boy who can spend hours throwing the ball for Milo. Mr P has taken all the guests up to the moors hawking and I am having a lazy afternoon, or I was until the BT engineer turned up. Asking me all sorts of technical questions about how many wires etc go out of the main box. I don't even know how many rooms there are let alone how many wires travel to them!

Anyway he's gone now so back to my lazy afternoon for which I just don't know what to do. Might have a sneaky nap, we all stayed up late last night having an extremely informative conversation about Prostate Cancer, definitely a conversation worth having as far as I am concerned...

A lot of cutlery - 26th August

Not sleeping very well at the moment, have moved into a room (maids quarters!) above the kitchen/Aga so like a little oven up there. Thought I would have a little siesta this afternoon to catch up and just as I was drifting off two bloomin big blue bottles decided to join me, so now I feel even more tired!

Popped to local Tesco this morning with passengers in my van, they were actually quite impressed with The Beast and not at all afraid! I hadn't been to a supermarket for so long I didn't quite know what to buy so ended up with multi packs of steak Macoys crisps and chocolate chip cookies.

Washed some dishes this morning and wondered if I would ever need so much cutlery after surviving in the van with one knife, fork and spoon.

Milo is still living in the van, it is soul destroying seeing him sitting in the passenger seat looking out the window no doubt waiting for me to jump in and start the engine. I took him out for a little drive this afternoon and we pulled up by a loch and he fell asleep quite content. I took advantage and phoned my bestie Sue for a catch up, which made me miss her even more. Milo and Me are both possibly feeling a little lost just now. Hopefully given time we will know where we belong...

Melted wellies - 27th August

This morning Mr P and I built a washing line, well we assembled one with some rather dodgy instructions with help from others. In total it took four of us about an hour but we are all now rather pleased with ourselves. We even, for some unknown reason, have a viewing chair for said washing line!

Then this afternoon I had the great pleasure of going onto the moors to hawk. A first for me and my female companion, and no doubt we won't be asked to return! It was an intriguing experience and I was rather kindly (or not) supplied with a midgy hat.

Basically for those who don't know (me included) we drive for miles over rugged moorland until we find a suitable spot then we all get out the vehicles and let the dogs off. They run around looking rather excited and then stop and point, literally, hence Pointer dogs :) Then we let the Hawk off the glove, hopefully with a fully functioning transmitter, and watch it fly off and above. Then the hawking man jumps up and down shouting out loud until the grouse jump up out of the heather. And that's when the hawk swoops down to catch the grouse. I do apologise for my rather ignorant description of this process! But it was really interesting, until I fell over in the bog, nearly lost a welly and got soaked in a downpour of rain.

We then all returned to the cottage and had beer and chocolate biscuits. But I stood too close to the fire and sadly melted my wellies.

Girls and guns - 30th August

Moved out of the maids quarters last night as getting far too hot being above the Aga and we are now in the main house. Noticed the difference in temperature straight away so no doubt will move back in the winter! Stupidly I forgot to tell Milo which room I was in and as he had eaten the contents of the left over party food out of the bin, he had a rather gruesome accident on the hall carpet during the night. Thankfully it had been all cleared up by Mr P by the time I woke up.

This afternoon we all got to do some rifle shooting. Milo had to watch all this from the van due to health and safety (crazy gun girls possibly shooting him accidentally) so I've just spent the last hour sitting in the van with him blasting out some tunes and pretending we were on a road trip...

Beer and cake - 2nd September

Had a couple of quiet days at the Big house. Monday did practically nothing, had a few hours on my own so had a sneaky siesta in the afternoon and woke up thinking I was at home, then realised I gave all that away months ago, moment of panic overcome by mopping the kitchen floor. Mr P cooked a beautiful leg of lamb for supper and we all had an early night. But I was awake most of the night due to the afternoon nap.

Tuesday Mr P had a haircut appointment in the town, so Missy L and I went along for the ride. Mr R had an unfortunate ankle injury so stayed home with ice packs and babysat Milo. Missy L and I wandered around the town in the pouring rain which took all of five minutes and then found a suitable establishment serving alcohol! Two beers and two cakes in and all was good. Mr P then found us and offered us the choice of going to the supermarket with him or staying for another beer. Obviously we chose the latter. After much girly chat we were collected by Mr P. We returned to the Big house and both collapsed in the drawing room in front of the fire with a book each and a large glass of red while Mr P cooked supper!

Today Missy L and I are contemplating whether or not to venture down to the boat house and take the boat out on the Loch. Neither of us have any experience of boats but hey ho why should that be a problem...

A sad day at the Big House - 4th September

A sad day in the Big house. My Missy L has left us. Mr P and I drove her to Inverness airport for her journey South. I did contemplate trying to steal her ticket or break her legs, but knew I had to let her go. The journey back to the Big house was long and quiet. I said to Mr P it felt like we had seen our child off to university, would she call us? when would she visit us? the Big house would feel so empty without her. Then on our return I realised I had the whole bottle of wine to myself and soon puckered up!

Mr P did try to cheer me up by taking me shopping in Inverness. Quite a nice city for wandering around. He bought me items of clothing ;) and some sort of waterproof shoes to wear, presumably for when I am hauling coal in from outside! Oh and he did buy me a full length mirror as there are none in the Big house and I haven't seen my legs for over two months. We walked by the river and saw the castle and then went for some lunch. Then we spent the next twenty minutes wandering around the multi-storey car park looking for the Big car!

So, now it's just me and a house full of males and that includes Milo who is a little unwell today :(He swallowed a fly and when trying to cough it up he emptied the entire contents of his stomach, yuk. He then spent the next hour curled up on my knee feeling rather sorry for himself. I felt like a mum again...

My new peeing technique - 5th September

As the nights get darker I am more aware of the lack of curtains in the Big house, more so in the bathrooms. Now I do appreciate we have no neighbours but people do possess binoculars and it seems all the toilets are positioned next to or nearby a window. I could close the shutters but that would involve removing all my products off the window sill. So I have adapted a technique of dropping my panties whilst practically sitting down!

Mr P went off hawking again today so I decided to fire up The Beast and take Milo to the beach. Sadly The Beast was not as keen and took quite a while to fire up.   Eventually I got going but the tide was right in and pretty rough, so we returned and settled for a walk around the garden.

Soon we will be fat - 7th September

Mr P was offered the opportunity of quarter of a cow from our farmer neighbour. He seemed to be deliberating this until I pointed out that he has four freezers one holding a mouldy punnet of strawberries and another a block of salted butter! Looking forward to our supply of very local Aberdeen Angus :)

Today I have scraped all the green slime away from the front gate. I am fed up stepping in it and nearly breaking my neck every time I step out of the car to open the gate. Mr P dismissed my idea of electric gates. At some point this week I am going to become an Aga supreme cook! I have a few recipe books and an Aga tip book. I am quite excited about the drop scones, the pancakes, the seven minute quick cake and tip number 9 about reviving stale bread. Yes, I can see it now, Mr P and I will soon be the fattest people in the village...

Alone with my mystery man - 10th September

Today is the first day Mr P and I have been alone in the Big house for about a month. We have no guests visiting for about a week. Gives us a chance to get to know each other properly or we could possibly end up murdering each other! I will keep you updated, unless I am the murdered one!

Tomorrow a photographer is coming to take photos for the Sunday Post this Sunday. They are doing a follow up story of Milo and Me and finding Mr P. The story will run mainly on me as Mr P is not keen to be splashed across the tabloids. And I respect his feelings on this. So they will probably photograph me and Milo minus my Mystery Man. I suggested he could hide in the background wearing a large hat, something like a Jack Vettriano picture...

Locked out the Big House - 12th September

The photographer for The Sunday Post turned up right on time and had a little scout about for suitable shots. He then enquired if I had any suitable attire for my country lifestyle, obviously my Nike anorak was not the look he was hoping for. Mr P saved the day and provided me with his Barbour jacket, tweed cap and walking stick! So off we went to the walled garden to begin with, where Milo decided to roll in a pile of fox pooh whilst being photographed, not a good look. I can't imagine what the pics will be like other than me looking like someone wearing her dad's clothes and Milo covered in s**t! Mr P said we have to go to the paper shop early tomorrow morning and buy every copy, for a moment I thought he was being sweet...

This morning I took Milo for his usual walk on the hill and when I got back to the Big house Mr P had locked the back door. I tried all the doors and windows to no avail.   Then I tried phoning him but no answer. I didn't know what to do next. I did actually check my van to see if he had dumped all my stuff into it. Eventually he came downstairs and found me in the garage, apparently he had gone for his shower thinking I was still in bed. So now I have been instructed to always take a door key.

Photo of me and Mr P - 17th September

Well I said I needed to spice my life up and I think I might have just done that. Mr P and I have just done an interview with the Daily Mail newspaper and we are appearing in Femail on Saturday. Mr P took a bit of persuading to 'reveal' himself but has agreed to go public. Tomorrow they are sending a photographer to do a shoot at the Big house. Sadly as it is such short notice they are unable to send the makeup artist or hairdresser, devastated. So I apologise in advance for my scruffy appearance. Mr P will of course be wearing his kilt attire, I will no doubt borrow his wax jacket. I was interviewed by the lovely Jenny Johnston and am a little concerned I may have had verbal diarrhea, so Mr P I apologise if I said too much!

Wow! - 19th September

Gosh what an exciting day! Of all my herbs it seems my basil is the fastest grower... Mwhaha! Seriously Lordy Lord what a day! When I clicked on my iPad my blog page seemed to be over reacting regarding viewing figures. I thought how odd? Then I opened the Mail online to see if I could find the story about Me and Mr P. I didn't have to look far! Jenny Johnston wrote a lovely article on us both.

Of all the comments, we are embracing the kind and encouraging ones and saying 'pooh to you' to the negative ones (which are hugely outweighed by the positives).   We are both quite overwhelmed by the response to our romance, and I am personally pleased with how much closer it has made us :) For the record Mr P is romantic and always puts my heated seat on in the car before his.

I really do need to thank all the guys responsible for our story, you know who you are! And apologise to anyone I have not managed to message today. And thank my family and Mr P's for dealing with our crazy whirlwind romance! And while I'm on the subject of thankyous, I just love the steak pies Mr P gets from Bews the local Butcher. Oh dear this reads like an Oscar acceptance speech haha!

Well next stage is we have been invited to appear on TV this week, yikes! I am seriously lacking in a change of wardrobe and haven't had my hair done since February (miss you Dave). But hey ho what you see is what you get with me. So I'm off to batten down the hatches and head to bed. Sweet dreams everyone, coz they do come true you know...

Spending Mr P's millions - 20th September

Question; can you have salad with dressing on the same plate as meat, veg and gravy? According to Mr P this is perfectly acceptable, according to me it's just plain wrong! Could this be our first argument in the Big house! Today has been much quieter than all the shenanigans of yesterday. The phone never stopped ringing and messages came from far and wide. I told Mr P that it didn't bother me that most people loved him and saw me as a gold digging ho! Of all the messages I've received throughout my adventure only one ever needed to reach me... And he did.

Miloandme and Mr P on TV - 21st September

Oh my word! Another crazy day at the Big house. ITV This Morning, with Philip and Holly have invited Mr P and Me to be interviewed on Wednesday!! Sadly Milo has to stay at the Big house :(Mr P has never watched this programme. I, however, am a massive fan. I do hope Gino is on :) (must remember to pack my pinny) This is all rather surreal for us both but we have decided to just try and be ourselves and go with the flow. We are both excited and nervous, well actually I am a screaming psychopath inside but am playing it down for Mr P! I am absolutely sure everybody will love Mr P and I will most likely get the usual unpleasant comments. But hey ho I am made of strong stuff.

Alice in Wonderland - 24th September

'This Morning' (see what I did there?! Haha) whilst walking Milo I found the biggest rabbit hole I've ever seen. I reckon if I changed my name to Alice I could climb in it! Back in the real world... I actually do feel like Alice in Wonderland. The last few days have been a whirlwind to say the least.

Mr P and I woke up really early on Wednesday and were so nervous we couldn't even stomach the fantastic cooked breakfast at our hotel (which bizarrely included peas!). We were collected by our driver and taken to the ITV studio where we were met by a lovely doorman by name. We were then taken straight to The Green Room (which does actually have a subtle green colour) and provided with lots of refreshments.   Then we were taken to 'makeup' much to the bemusement of Mr P! I felt like a celebrity sitting in the makeup chair and all the girls were so lovely. One of them asked for my list of unsuccessful men!

Mr P was slightly disappointed Sue Ellen was not in the studio but was compensated by getting to meet Holly. I was chuffed chatting to Rylan, he is so sweet. And Harry and Dave of Rich Landscapes were adorable young men as was their 3 year old black lab. Was funny seeing The Osmond brothers too! But I must admit Phillip was my favourite :)

The actual interview went so quickly and apparently we were caught on camera kissing! I haven't seen that bit. I must say everyone at ITV was just so nice to us both, I can't thank them enough. Even when our driver took us out the building people at the gate shouted, 'that's Nicci!' And even at the airport two lovely ladies approached us and said they'd watched us on telly. We have received so so many messages and even Milo has messages. I could write about this forever, but I am still on cloud nine!

I Love... - 25th September

I love that Mr P looks like the hunny monster first thing in the morning. I love in the morning when Milo dives on my bed and throws his back on top of me and headbutts me. I love that my mum cried when she saw me on the television. I love that my son saw me on television and has not 'yet' disowned me. I love that my sister listens to all that I have to say and always sounds interested. I love that my best friend cannot hear from me for ages but pick up on our last conversation. I am so lucky in love that Kylie Minogue would be jealous!

I am extremely excited today as my best friend, of 25 years, is coming to stay at the Big house for the weekend.

The moon is mine - 28th September

Today I'm feeling really down. My best friend left the Big house yesterday and as I said to Mr P she was the first guest we'd had that I didn't have to be introduced to. It was such a lovely weekend and was over far too quickly. I've spent so long at the Big house trying to fit in and feel at home. This weekend was a little different to that, I felt like I was welcoming my friend into my home. And now she's gone, grhh!

My mood was slightly lifted this morning by the beautiful sunrise I pictured. Sadly I missed the Blood Moon. One of my favourite songs is The Moon is Mine by Fairground Attraction, never fails to uplift me...

We were on a break - 29th September

This will be my last blog entry for a while. Mr P has requested some peace and quiet from the limelight and has suggested I take a blog holiday. For a minute I thought that he meant an exotic Caribbean beach holiday.

I know for a fact I will miss my blog dreadfully and will no doubt have some sort of withdrawal symptoms. I'm sure my sister will be inundated with my phone calls and text messages and pray for the blog to return. I am really rather sad...

Chapter 22

I was heading towards Perth where I was to meet my mum. She was originally going to be staying at the Big House with me and Mr P. I was so disappointed my family had never got to meet Mr P, other than seeing him on TV. I was sad they didn't get to visit us at the Big House.

For now my mum had booked a hotel for us which was also dog friendly. And I was actually looking forward to some mother-daughter advice.

Driving away from Caithness I took in the vast openness of it all. This time I didn't quite notice the big wind farms they now seemed to belong to the stunning landscape. The Berriedale dips felt different, this time embracing The Beast and not terrifying it. The coastal fog had lifted and the sun was shining. Milo had curled up on the couch behind me and the radio tunes were uplifting. Everything was going my way. But it wasn't. I felt so empty and so sad. I felt like a failure and could hear what my mum had said in the beginning "what will you do when you get back?". And here I was, going back, a failure.

I reflected on what I had achieved so far. I'd met so many wonderful people from all walks of life. I'd had the good fortune to view the most amazing landscapes, exploding sunrises and calming sunsets. I'd paddled in lagoons on deserted beaches, scrambled up cliffs to view the ocean, discovered hidden fairy-tale castles in the woods, skimmed stones across glass-like lochs and slept peacefully under the stars in a golden silence. I'd done all this because I wanted to. I'd done all this because I could. I was certainly not ready to stop or go back.

I arrived in Perth and was met with a much needed mum hug. With the added bonus of a Chinese meal and a shopping trip. Mum bought me a beautiful pair of black, suede high heeled boots and two pairs of knee high thermal socks. She also bought Milo a cute padded rain coat, he didn't seemed so impressed. Although he was impressed with the open buckets full of dog treats scattered about the store, I'm not sure how many he managed to eat but the shop assistant was kind enough to just take payment for one.

We headed off to our pet friendly hotel in Scone and bedded down for the night. The next morning at breakfast I decided to warm my croissant through the rotating toaster. Big mistake. Within seconds there were large flames coming off the croissant as it slowly rotated through. I managed to pull it out with the tongs, place the black charred remains on my plate next to the butter and jam and discreetly sit down. Apparently I hadn't been so discreet as the next morning a large sign had been placed next to the toaster stating 'not suitable for croissants'.

After a few days holed up in motels with Milo and my mum, and beginning to feel like Thelma and Louise, mum had to return home. My mum assured me I had not failed, everyone loved me and whatever I decided to do was fine by her. I needed to hear this. I still didn't know what to do next but I did feel slightly more positive. I had no plan in mind so chose to head to a camp-site near Stirling.

I chose a parking spot furthest away from other motor homes with enough open space for Milo to run around on. Once we were pitched up we walked to the restaurant I had spotted near the entrance. The door bore a sign saying 'pets welcome' and it seemed pretty quiet. I opened the door and walked in. Here I was met by a member of staff who said to me "no dogs allowed".

I've never been very good with confrontation and literally just walked out and silently cried all the way back to the van

Back in the van I rummaged through my sparse food cupboard and came up with a combination of tinned curry, dried pasta and tinned rice pudding. Not bad considering.

I then received a telephone call from an unknown number. It was a journalist wanting to write my side of the story as to why my relationship had ended with Mr P. I explained to him that our reasons were personal at which point he started to offer payment for my story. The more I refused the higher the payment got. When he finally realised I wasn't going to talk he informed me that a version of events would be published in the media with or without my input. And apparently there was nothing I could do to stop this.

And true to his word the next day the 'breakup' was printed. National newspapers had headlines quoting 'it's over', 'blogger Nicci ends it with Mr P', 'Nicci and Milo back on the road'. Yet again there was a bizarre fascination with my life. The media articles were out there and I could deal with that. What hurt was the comments people had subsequently written in response. There were thousands of them online, mainly anonymous, and mainly scathing. Mr P was in short the victim and I was a slut, a gold digger, a tart with a mattress on her back and numerous other cruel and nasty names. These comments were made by people who didn't know me, had never met me and knew nothing about me. But they all decided they had the right to judge me. Their comments hurt but I told myself that if they actually met me in person they would surely like me. That helped me sleep at night.

Reflecting, Loch Tay...

The following morning, having received a message from a journalist claiming to know where I was, I decided to drive to my best friend's house. I needed sanctuary as I'd had visions of a journalist hidden in a tree with a long lens camera taking pictures of me picking my nose.

Sue, as usual, welcomed me with open arms and a large bottle of Pinot. She provided a comfy bed for me and Milo and a big bubbly bath. She even lit calming candles around the bathtub. We sat up late into the night discussing my breakup and what to do next. Sue was convinced Mr P had been influenced by so called friends on the path of our relationship. I was just saddened we hadn't been able to make it work and didn't want to blame anyone. Relationships end every day, mine was no different, other than complete strangers were stating their opinions.

We did have a giggle that one national newspaper had written the final straw was when Sue came to visit the Big house. Sue will now always be known as my final straw.

Staying with Sue and her partner was welcoming. But it was difficult to not feel jealous of her loving and happy relationship. She'd met the man of her dreams and witnessing their display of affections was not where I wanted to be.

From day one of my adventure I'd received various messages from complete strangers. Many from people inviting me to visit them on my travels. Now I was reading a message from a gentleman named Alistair. He'd read my blog and said he felt sorry for me. He'd recently gone through a relationship breakup and understood how I felt. He told me if I wanted to hide away from it all and get my head together he had a place for me to stay. No strings attached. Secluded location near the beach on the West Coast of Scotland.

Once again I could hear my mother's voice.

"He might be a murderer."

Me, "He might not be."

Alistair continued to message me even offering to meet me, with Sue, in a public place first. He seemed genuine. My gut instinct told me he was safe. So I followed my gut instinct and took him up on his offer of sanctuary.

Yet again Milo was packed into The Beast and off we went. Milo was getting quite used to our travels. He recognised certain routines. If he saw me coiling in the long blue electric cable, it didn't matter where he was or what he was doing, he knew we were leaving and would jump straight into the van. As soon as the engine started he would take up residence on the bench behind me and rest his head on my right shoulder. He loved taking in the views of the open road as much as I did. And boy were the views stunning just now. I do believe Autumn is my favourite season. Especially so in Scotland.

The sun was lower but appeared to have a warmer glow to it. All the leaves were turning golden and the fields were the brightest of green. Rivers and streams flowed furiously, glistening in the sunshine. Rainbows appeared frequently and span across hills and mountains convincing me I truly could find the end of the rainbow. I felt happy and blessed sitting high up in my driver seat milking the scenery.

I saw a hitch-hiker on the road and swear he pulled his thumb back in when he saw me. No doubt he'd read my story and thought it safer to walk.

We stopped overnight in Killin at Maragowan campsite. A place we'd already visited and enjoyed. People talk of driving route NC500 to appreciate Scotland, my route so far resembled a game of snakes and ladders. We'd zigzagged our way through Scotland.

Killin was peaceful. We took a walk into the village crossing the multi-arched stone bridge over the Falls of Dochart. We walked all day and rested on the banks of Loch Tay. Well I say rested, Milo swam for miles in the loch.   That night I cooked a favourite meal of mince and mash with Milo enjoying the leftovers. I slept peacefully that night. That is until I awoke in the middle of the night, opened my eyes and saw the large figure of a man standing in my kitchen area. I desperately scrambled under my pillow to find my claw hammer, banging my head on the cabin ceiling as I did so. This in turn woke Milo who started barking furiously at our intruder. I eventually found my claw hammer by which time my eyes had adjusted, and I could see our murderer was in fact my black coat hanging from the sky light. I decided that night to stop reading scary books before bed.

In the morning I telephoned Alistair and said I was hoping to take up his offer of sanctuary if it was still open. He was quite enthusiastic and gave me directions to meet him in a car-park about an hour's drive away. Our drive blessed us with scenery of The Trossachs national park and the sun was shining. Once again, I felt privileged to be driving these stunning routes on such a beautiful day. We stopped off at The Green Welly Stop, which was surprisingly a hive of activity for being in such a quiet location.

I didn't quite know where Alistair lived, he'd said it was near Lochgilphead and I was to follow him from the car-park. When I arrived at the car-park, which was more of a lay by, there was Alistair. He was sitting on the back of his pick-up truck his legs swinging and chewing a blade of grass. I pulled up beside him and he trotted over and opened my driver door. This of course set Milo off into his killer dog barking mode. I, at this point, had a fleeting thought of what I was actually doing. I had no idea where I was, I had no idea who Alistair was, I had no idea where he was taking me and no one knew of my whereabouts. It was, as such, a fleeting thought as my gut instinct soon kicked in and I reminded myself I'd lived this long so far.

Alistair jumped into his pickup and said follow me. I started off trying to store the route, in reverse, visually into my memory. After about ten minutes, many turns and many bends in the road I had no idea of my whereabouts. I was at this point just desperately trying to keep up with him. He drove like a bat out of hell. I don't think he realised how slow my Beast travelled. He had to keep pulling over and wait for me to catch up.

We drove for at least thirty minutes until we reached his house. His house was nestled at the bottom of a mountain overlooking the coast. He lived in one of the farm properties and was surrounded by fields full of sheep. It was a glorious location. His home wasn't quite country cottage more of a 1970's bungalow. His living arrangements were typical of man living in the sticks on his own. Sparse furniture, no pictures, bare kitchen cupboards, mismatching décor and curiously no television.

I was shown to my room and informed the bedding was clean on today and an electric blanket was on the mattress. Alistair then went to prepare us a meal for the evening. Liver and onions. Yuk. I politely declined, pretending I'd stopped for a big lunch en route, and then sat there feeling very hungry for most of the night. Our evening was spent sitting by the fire and Alistair telling me of his broken heart. He was, it appeared, very lonely. I was quite tired so went to bed early and ate crisps under the duvet.

Next morning I took Milo down to the beach. Unfortunately the tide was out and the beach was a mass of seaweed. Seaweed scares me. Ever since I was a child I have believed seaweed can bite you. I still believe this to be true.

We headed back to the house and I sat on the back step with a pot of coffee and my book. Milo was happy to play catch with the tennis ball and Alistair had gone off to chop wood. That is until he suddenly appeared on the step behind me with a large axe in his hand.

"You look sad, Nicci, you look like you need a hug." he said as he lurched forward and threw his arms around me. It was a prolonged hug which was followed by "you need one of my massages." as he proceeded to knuckle my shoulders. Awkward, I thought as I sat there quite rigid. I didn't want to offend Alistair but I did feel quite uncomfortable. I think he sensed this and went off to the kitchen to make himself a coffee.

He was gone quite a while and I wondered if I'd been unkind. After all, this man had opened up his home to me and maybe I was being ungrateful. But I'm not very good with space invasion. I wasn't attracted to him and I certainly hadn't flirted. And now my gut instinct was telling me that Alistair wanted more than a house guest. I needed to be careful how I handled this situation.

As I was contemplating how I was going to do this Alistair, once again, appeared from nowhere. This time carrying a large petrol operated chainsaw. The noise was deafening and set Milo barking in competition. I froze momentarily, a scene in my head of me being chopped into small pieces and scattered amongst the seaweed. Then Alistair hopped over the fence shouting out he was off to chop some more wood. I watched him head down to the bottom field and then I phoned Pip.

Pip quite rightly said if I felt uncomfortable I should leave. Alistair hadn't really done anything wrong other than misread me. Trouble was I didn't know where to go. I didn't have enough money to keep travelling. I didn't want to go home added with the fact that I didn't have a home. And I certainly wasn't ready to end my adventure.

I sat there, on the step, watching Alistair in the distance chopping wood, the faint sound of the chainsaw drifting up the field. Milo was snoozing by my feet and the sun was shining bright. I could see the shepherds on the mountainside bringing down the sheep. I could smell the sea air and feel the warm breeze on my face. I felt like I was in heaven and hell. Why couldn't Alistair be my Mr Perfect?

Later in the day I opened my emails. Mr L had written to me. Dear Mr L. Mr L and I had been corresponding since the beginning of my journey. He lived in San Pedro near Belize and had spent the whole summer trying to convince me not to go to Scotland.

"Why go to cold, rainy Scotland when you could come to hot, sunny San Pedro?" He'd written so often.

Mr L had lived in San Pedro for many years with his dogs and owned hotels on the island. He wrote his own blog and had enthusiastically followed mine. Today he was writing to me with concern. He'd read my blog and could see how unhappy I was. He brutally wrote " last chance, I'm booking you a ticket, get your arse over here!"

Hmm I thought. OK.

Extracts from my blog miloandme6.blogspot.com

Just Milo and me - 7th October

'I'm wondering to myself how on earth do I write this today... I'm wondering how to explain a bucket full of emotions in one blog entry... I'm wondering how I will be perceived... So I will just write like I always have. This is me and I am no longer with Mr P. It's over. Finito. Ended. Gone.

It really is an unusual story and one that I am unable, at this point, to share in full. Mr P was a good person as am I. Sadly we couldn't be good together.   Sometimes it's just as simple as the person you thought you knew just isn't... But you think to yourself I can deal with this, I can make this work, I won't give up. Then you realise you're not coping, it's not working, and you have to stop. I chose to end this for both our sakes.

I truly thought I had found my fairytale ending. I was so happy for a moment in time. I did believe I nearly had it all. Oh how wrong was I...

Relationships break down every day for one reason or another.   Mine has been no different and yet so different I don't think I'll ever be able to understand it. The people close to me have an insight to a small percent of what happened, the rest is just a mess in my head! So I'll just box it all up and figure it out one day...

Good friends and good wine - 9th October

I'm now quite content laughing at the comments in the press saying that I look like his mother or have slept my way around Scotland because I know what his mother looks like and Scotland ain't that big.

Messages of support and love are still pouring in and I am so grateful for all the moral support. Milo and Me are really very lucky to have so many good friends.

So Milo and Me have holed up for a few days with good friends and good wine. We have received an extremely kind offer, offering us sanctuary for as long as we need on a beach. Obviously given my previous folly this offer requires serious deliberation! My blog seems to grow arms and legs... So for now Milo And Me are keeping our feet firmly on the ground and taking life an hour at a time...

No more hitch hikers - 11th October

Just after lunch I left my besties with an enormous hug to keep me going on the road. I'm now pitched up for the night in a rather peaceful spot but have no phone or internet reception. So I have wandered down to the local village pub and am taking advantage of the free Wi-Fi before it gets dark. I was sitting in a very quiet lounge area until two gentlemen arrived and are now having a rather loud discussion about the amount of cushions on the sofa. Think it's time to head back to the van and tuck myself in for the night...

A sheep or a shepherd - 13th October

Tonight I have travelled along an extremely long, narrow and winding road and have arrived at a safe destination on the coast.   am staying with a stranger but I do believe strangers are friends you just haven't met yet...

I am feeling a bit sorry for myself today. It's my son's birthday and all my family are together and I'm up here wandering around watching sheep. I wish I was with them today. I need to seriously get my head together and decide what I intend to do with my life. I seem to be at a crossroads and just cannot decide which way to turn and with my sense of direction it's likely to be the wrong way! I could possibly train Milo and become a shepherd...

Chapter 23

Decision made. San Pedro it was then. Now all I had to do was escape from my chainsaw massacre. I could still see Alistair in the distance, his chainsaw confidently waving through the air as he swung down on the tree logs. I figured he'd be there a while longer so decided to gather all my belongings and pack up my van. Ready for my escape. I knew I was overreacting and Alistair obviously had no intention of stopping me from leaving. But I don't like confrontation and decided a short, sharp exit was my best plan.

I was sitting back on the step when once again Alistair appeared from nowhere. He sat on the step behind me and began to massage my shoulders. I immediately jumped up and asked if he'd like a coffee.

"Are you OK, Nicci?" he asked. "You seem a little sad."

"Oh I am, Alistair." I replied. "I'm missing my family, I'm missing Mr P and I'm missing being on the road." I paused, "I think it's time I moved on, Alistair."

"Oh" he said "when are you thinking of leaving?"

"Err, now." I stuttered

"What? Like right now?"

"Err, yes. When I make a decision I like to just get on with it. It's been so lovely spending these few days with you but it is time for me to leave."

I grabbed Milo's tennis ball and headed round to the front of the house where my van sat with the keys in the ignition. Milo duly followed and jumped in his seat. I started the engine and put it into reverse.

Alistair then opened the passenger door and insisted he check my oil and water levels before I left. I sat there watching him under my bonnet wondering if he had now decided to cut my brake pipes rather than chop me up with the chainsaw. Get a grip! I chastised myself.

Alistair slammed down the bonnet and I reversed out of the drive and onto the bumpy lane. He stood at the gate watching us head down the long lane towards the main road. As I hooked a sharp left onto the main road my passenger door flew open and my handbag shot out the door onto the road. I had to slam on my breaks, hit the hazard warning lights, jump out the van and walk back down the road to retrieve my handbag. I could still see Alistair watching in the distance probably wondering if I'd changed my mind and was heading back.

A couple of miles down the road I pulled into a lay-by and phoned Pip. I told her I'd left and now had no internet connection. Today was Wednesday, my last email from Mr L said he had booked me a ticket from Heathrow for this Friday. He also chose to inform me that I should know he had met a lady and was in a relationship. I was somewhere on the west coast of Scotland and had to drive hundreds of miles to get Milo to my mum's house and then catch a flight from Manchester to Heathrow. I asked Pip if she could go online and book me the cheapest flight available to Heathrow. And also liaise with Mr L online for me regarding my travel plans.

I followed the signs for Glasgow, if I could get to Glasgow then I would be familiar with the route back to my mums I figured. But it was getting late and I was tired. I decided to find a safe place to stop and bed down for a few hours.

At 4am my alarm was screaming in my ear and Milo was bouncing from couch to couch. It was still dark and Milo was a little reluctant to go outside for his wee. After a little persuasion he did his wee and then we jumped in the van and headed South. Milo was extremely confused, travelling in the dark, and chose to sit behind me all the way with his head on my shoulder. Maybe he sensed we were heading for a separation?

Chapter 24

I arrived back on the Wirral at about 8 am having not stopped all the way. My Beast was no doubt exhausted and looking forward to a well-earned rest. I drove straight to Pip's where she threw her arms round me and then put the kettle on. She filled me in on all the correspondence from Mr L and gave me the information for my travel plans. Then she went off for a shower. I was sitting in the kitchen when Pip came out the shower. I was engrossed in my emails and she sat quietly next to me. After a while she looked at me and asked

"Why are you here?"

I laughed and replied "I'm going to San Pedro."

She didn't respond and I carried on with my reading.

A little while later Pip looked at me, rather vaguely, and asked again, "Why are you here?"

"Duh! I'm going to San Pedro you numpty" I replied.

"Oh." she said.

By now my mum had arrived and we were busy chatting about my travel plans. Pip was still very quiet and Mum asked her if she was OK?

"Why is Nicci here?" she asked my mum

"She's going to South America, Love." Mum answered

"Oh, when did she get here?" Pip enquired with a vacant look in her eyes.

Mum and I exchanged glances. Something wasn't right. We put our coats on and drove to the doctor's surgery. Given Pip's medical history we were not taking any chances. The receptionist booked her in for a 5pm appointment so we decided to go and get some lunch. Once in the restaurant Pip headed to the toilets and was gone some time. Mum and I both agreed she wasn't 'quite right' and were both rather worried at her strange behaviour. When she returned from the toilet she asked why we were all here? At this point I said to Mum that we should just drive straight to A&E. Mum agreed.

Pip was pretty much seen straight away. The whole day was spent running tests and by the evening the doctor concluded that Pip had had some sort of seizure. They couldn't determine if this was in any way linked to her past brain haemorrhage but was more than likely a one off due to stress. She was discharged and told to take it easy and a follow up appointment would be booked with a consultant. The doctor stressed to Pip that she should not try to recall any memory from after her shower that morning, as the path to that memory was lost forever. Pip had basically 'lost' a whole day of her life. It was hard for Pip to not try and recall the events of the day and it was fun for me to wind her up. She didn't believe me when I said she'd offered to pay for my London flight.

I was in two minds as to whether or not I should be flying off to South America in the morning but everyone, including Pip, convinced me I should. Although Pip was slowly returning to her normal self it was now nearing midnight and I hadn't even packed. My flight was departing at 7am.

I've always been a bit of a list and planner type girl. Packing for a holiday would be done with military precision. Not tonight. I literally grabbed all my summer clothes and just threw them in a suitcase, unfolded. Passport in handbag and Dollars would be purchased at the airport.

Milo and I slept on my mum's couch for about two hours before I had to head off to Manchester airport. I was inconsolable saying goodbye to Milo. I felt like I was chopping my right arm off. Mum assured me he would be absolutely fine and spoilt rotten by everybody, but it still broke my heart to leave him. I'd only ever left him to go to the shops of late. So I gave him the biggest hug ever and said "I'm just going to the shops baby, see you later." as he stared at my hands waiting for his 'I'm going to the shops biscuit'.

Chapter 25

My journey ahead consisted of five flights. Manchester to London. London to Detroit. Detroit to Atlanta. Atlanta to Belize. Belize to San Pedro. Not a problem for an ex air-hostess but a long journey nonetheless. The most difficult aspect was travelling without Milo. He'd been my constant travelling companion since we'd started our adventure, it felt odd him not being by my side.

This was such a different class of travel for me. I was being waited on hand and foot. There was no map reading, no getting lost and no difficult three-point turns. Free drinks, hot food and movies were provided on most of my flights. And yet I still missed my Beast.

Detroit was lonesome. I had an eleven-hour turnaround and it was late at night. As I was unable to check-in until 6 am I found myself alone in the arrivals hall. For such a huge airport there was a massive lack of people. Apart from a couple of guys polishing the floors I appeared to be the only person here. None of the cafés were open and all I could find was one vending machine selling a small selection of snacks. I found myself a safe seating area, tied my suitcase to my leg with my scarf and tried to settle down for the night using my handbag as a pillow. I drifted off intermittently and always awoke with a panic of 'where's Milo?'

After a long night I was eventually able to check in and access the wonders of Detroit airport. Coffee. Food. Happy.

Detroit to Atlanta was a smooth and pleasant flight, as was Atlanta to Belize. I had a full row of seats to myself on both flights and was presented with a full in-flight service. I watched movies, drank wine and ate ice-cream. Pure luxury all the way. Disembarking in Belize was an eye-opener. This was not a modern airport. The waiting area for my onward flight to San Pedro reminded me of an old-fashioned railway station waiting room with hard wooden benches positioned in rows. The shops were like something from a back-street bazaar. The toilets left a lot to be desired. Fortunately, I was not there for long before my next flight departure was announced, or rather shouted out.

As I walked toward my aircraft I regretted my choice of clothing I'd worn since leaving my mum's house nearly thirty hours earlier. Thick black trousers, high heeled black, suede boots, knitted jumper and leather jacket. The sweat was trickling down the sides of my face and my feet felt like elephant's feet. Looking at the small aircraft in front of me I felt sorry for whoever sat next to me, I stank so much I didn't even want to sit next to me.

The flight was full. Captain, first officer and five passengers. I'd never flown in a light aircraft before and was quite excited. That is until we hit the storm.

How we managed to stay airborne I'll never know. We bounced around in that storm like a paper plane. The storm was quite horrendous and had flooded most of San Pedro. Looking down at the land it reminded me of paddy fields, not quite the golden sandy beaches I'd been expecting.

We hit the runway in San Pedro and skidded to a stop. The engine was shut down, the Captain jumped out and helped us passengers off the aircraft. I was then pointed in the direction of the terminal building.

And there was Mr L, awaiting my arrival. He was dressed in T-shirt and shorts and was barefoot. He grabbed my suitcase and said 'follow me' We then clambered into a golf buggy and drove off. The streets were flooded. It was like driving through fast flowing rivers. The rain was whipping my face through the open sides of the buggy, which was actually a welcome feeling in my sweaty condition.

Within minutes we had arrived at Mr L's hotel, which was Pedro's Inn, a hostel. A barefooted young man greeted us and lifted my suitcase off the back of the buggy. I watched them both wade through the foot-deep water toward the reception area. At this point I decided to remove my high heeled black suede boots, roll up my trousers and followed them, barefoot.

The whole building was at least a foot deep in water and was being pumped out, with a machine, into the street. All the furniture was piled on top of tables and various people were desperately trying to brush the water out from the building.

Mr L grabbed a key from the reception desk and said 'follow me' We waded back through the water and headed up a staircase, along a balcony and arrived at my new home for the foreseeable. From my balcony, Mr L pointed out his residence across the way and said 'pop over when you've freshened up'.

As soon as Mr L had left I threw myself on the bed and just lay there. The wooden ceiling fan whirring above my head sent down a welcoming breeze and the white cotton sheets felt good on my skin. I scanned my room. The whole room was clad in wood. I had a double bed, two bedside tables, a small TV and a clothes rail with four coat hangers. In the far corner was a small sink with a small mirror above. To my right was a bathroom housing a shower and toilet. Outside I had my own balcony, the main road ran just across the way but didn't seem too busy. This was perfect I thought to myself.

I lay there, quite still, reflecting on the last 72 hours. I'd charged out of Scotland, reached the Wirral in record time, spent a whole day in A&E and then flown halfway across the world to stay in an unfamiliar territory with a complete stranger. Mr L didn't seem too pleased to see me. I told myself he was just stressed, what with the storm damage to his property, I was properly an inconvenience he didn't really need at the moment. Hopefully the friendliness I'd felt in his emails would resume soon.

I stood under the hot shower and felt all the stickiness fall from my body. I put on some clean clothes, brushed my hair and headed over to Mr L's residence.

Mr L's door was wide open and the TV was blasting out. He was sprawled across the couch with two mobile phones, one to each ear. He motioned me to sit on the couch opposite. His two telephone conversations seemed heated, there was much swearing. Then he jumped up and said we should go to his other property. I duly followed.

His other property was a luxurious hotel complex, Caribbean Villas, on the beach, just five minutes down the river, I mean road. We headed straight to his Amber beach bar and the barman handed us Jäger bombs and beers. I was tired, hungry and suffering from jet-lag so this alcoholic beverage went straight to my head. After many more Jäger bombs and being introduced to the other two people in the bar, one of whom was a gentleman I'd sat next to on the light aircraft, we headed back to the hostel. Mr L hadn't said much to me all evening other than offering me the choice of staying at the beach hotel or the hostel. The thought of moving that night didn't appeal to me so I chose to remain at the hostel.

Back at the hostel Mr L instructed me to head to the bar where he would join me shortly. I, at this point, could barely stand and excused myself to retire to bed.

I slept like a baby that night. About fourteen hours in total. Before I'd even opened my eyes, I was aware Milo was not with me. A sudden sadness washed over me. I missed him so much already, it hurt.

As I lay there I was aware of a rather loud noise coming from outside. I got up and stepped outside onto my balcony. That's when I discovered the main road I'd seen last night was in fact the airport runway. Small aircraft were taking off and landing practically below my feet. Fortunately, it wasn't such a busy airport and provided some light entertainment.

I got dressed and headed over to reception to find Mr L. As soon as I stepped outside I was aware of how heavy the air was. It was such a moist atmosphere and I felt I was struggling to catch a breath. Such a difference from Scotland where every breath was so sharp and fresh. It took me a good few days before I felt I could actually breathe normally, the bonus being my skin required not a drop of moisturiser cream in this moist climate.

On entering Mr L's office I found him at his desk, once again with a phone to each ear and still shouting obscenities. He indicated the chair and motioned me to sit with a wave of his hand. He was barking instructions to every staff member who entered and still seemed angry and stressed. Not surprising, I thought, what with all this flood damage.

He hung up one of the telephones and then threw a fifty-dollar bill and a key at me and said "take a golf buggy and go get yourself some breakfast in the town." I duly obeyed.

Outside there was a line of four golf buggy's and I had no idea which one my key would operate. Added to which, I had no idea quite how they operated. I decided to walk into town.

Wading through the water ridden streets in my pumps I decided to stop off and buy a pair of flip-flops with my breakfast money. Fifty dollars for breakfast seemed a bit excessive. Walking out the shop, wearing my new two-dollar flip-flops, the heavens opened. I took refuge in the nearest wooden shack café. I was the only customer and was greeted by a very friendly Turkish waiter. He brought my coffee over and sat next to me.

"You are a beautiful lady, why are you alone?" he asked

I explained I was staying with a friend and was more than happy to be alone. He then asked me if I would like some marijuana with my coffee. I politely declined, paid for my one-dollar coffee and bid him farewell.

I headed back to the hostel, stopping off at a supermarket to buy crisps and chocolate. I hadn't really thought all this through, I thought. I was in South America staying with a gentleman who seemed none too pleased to see me and I had no money. I certainly didn't foresee Mr L throwing fifty dollars bills at me every day. What should I do? I thought. I had an open return ticket, provided by Mr L, so could therefore leave whenever I wanted to. But return to what? There was no going back to Mr P. I decided I would stick it out. Surely things could only improve?

Back at the hostel I gave Mr L his change, which he told me to keep. He told me to put all my bar and food bills in his name at both his establishments and then asked me, "Can you cook Yorkshire puddings?" "Err, yes." I replied. "Good. Arsenal are playing on Sunday and I have twenty friends coming for a Sunday dinner. You're on Yorkshire pudding duty." He then proceeded to take another phone call and seemed to forget I was in the room.

Sunday started with a loud knock on my door. It was one of the bar staff telling me I was to make my way over to Mr L's residence at midday to make the Yorkshire puddings. I got dressed and headed over. There was nobody there at Mr L's, the door was open and I went in to the kitchen. There I found two dozen eggs and a bag of flour on the counter. I then spent an age trying to find bowls, whisks, milk and cooking trays. Another twenty minutes was spent trying to figure out how to switch on the oven. Having been unable to find any weighing scales I took a gamble and guessed all measurements.

After nearly two hours of chaos I removed my Yorkshire pudding tray from the oven. I was presented with a large, square, flat lump of batter.

It would have to do, I thought. I cut it up into smaller squares and headed to the bar.

I could hear the party had started. I could see, through the window, about twenty people all sitting round a big table digging in to a roast dinner. Minus the Yorkshire pudding. The thought of walking in there terrified me. Although I'm not actually shy, I'm a classic introvert. Certain situations wobble me. One being walking into a room full of people I barely know. But the hot tray was beginning to burn my fingers so I had to go in.

As soon as I walked in Mr L shouted "At last! The Yorkshire pudding."

I placed the tray in the middle of the table and took up a seat on the end. Everyone appeared to know each other and were all deep in conversation. I sat there, observing them struggling to chew threw my Yorkshire pudding. I overheard one gentleman state 'it's rather meaty.'

I had failed to impress Mr L with my Yorkshire pudding so I was more than relieved when Arsenal won the match.

Chapter 26

The next few days I spent wandering around the town or hanging out at the beach bar. Sunbathing was not an option since it rained constantly. The grey-brown sea water, I was told, was normally aquamarine blue. The storm was still lurking and the damage was apparent, having washed up some gruesome items onto the beach. Every day I watched the staff combing the sand in front of their hotels removing the washed-up drudge. As every morning it reappeared.

One particular night I was awoken by the storm above me. The rain was horrendous and hammered on my tin roof. The thunder was so loud and shook me in my bed. I peeped out of the window and could see the fork lightning just above. This terrified me so much. I was in a wooden building with a tin roof. I had visions of the lightning striking the roof and burning my building down. I was so scared I packed a small bag ready for my imminent evacuation. No such evacuation occurred. The storm passed and just left more flood water for Mr L to pump out.

It seemed the storm had passed. The sun was shining and even Mr L seemed brighter. He told me he'd secured a contract with the British Army and they were using his hotel and hostel for their R & R breaks over the forthcoming weeks. They were currently in the jungle training the Belize Army and had been for six weeks. Mr L was foreseeing a tidy profit on his bar takings. I was foreseeing MEN!

It was late in the night and I couldn't sleep. The heat was unbearable and the hum of the air-conditioning was keeping me awake. I'd stepped out onto my balcony through the sliding doors, un-wedging the curtain pole I'd improvised as a lock on my unlockable door and was taking in the peacefulness of the night sky. Until I heard a commotion below me. I looked down and saw a man falling out of a golf buggy. He staggered to his feet and was swearing, loudly, in an American accent, at the driver.

He did attempt to punch the driver but just swiped the air and fell to the ground. He managed to pick himself up and then spent the next ten minutes trying to climb the staircase, bouncing off the walls, before reaching his room. The room next to mine. I heard one further, loud bang and then nothing. He must have passed out.

Late the next morning I'd gone to reception to choose a reading book and was returning to my oh so cool air-conditioned room. American boy was sitting at a table, outside reception, with his head in his hands. He was surrounded by some sort of snorkelling equipment.

"Good morning." I said "How's your head?"

"Hey, not great." he replied "I had a way too heavy drinking session last night and was then ripped off for a few hundred dollars by my driver. Now I've slept in and missed my pick up to go scuba diving."

"Oh dear, poor you." I said "Can you rearrange the dive?"

"Hey, there's always tomorrow!" he replied cheerily.

"Fancy joining me at the beach bar?" he asked.

American boy was about an age with my son and had such a positive outlook on life. We spent many hours and many beers at the beach bar over the coming days. He only managed to wake early enough for one scuba dive as he spent most nights having one more bourbon and one more 'smoke'.

My day to day mainly consisted of walking into town for morning coffee, lying on the beach watching the world go by, lunch and beers at the beach bar with American boy and evenings spent in my room watching US TV on Netflix.

I didn't really fit in here in San Pedro. I wasn't a young hip, backpacking scuba diver. I wasn't one of the retired locals and I wasn't half of one of the many honeymoon couples. I was a middle-aged woman relying on the hospitality of the local Peter Stringfellow. I couldn't wait for the army to arrive.

The next day I chose to take a short-cut down to the beach. Here I met Todd the Rasta Man. He was sitting on a wall with his pit-bull terrier, named Claire. We struck up a conversation, I told him about Milo, he told me about 'the spirit of the flesh'. I had no idea what he was talking about. He invited me to go back to his house and indulge in 'the herbal drugs' I politely declined and went on my way.

I then spotted a clothes shop. I headed over to take a peek inside. But it wasn't a clothes shop, on closer inspection it was actually someone's house, with their washing hung on a clothes line in such abundance and ever so neat. I wandered on, stopping at a fruit stall on the roadside. Here I bought apple flavoured bananas. They looked exactly like a banana but tasted exactly like an apple. My brain was so confused I felt like I'd inhaled Todd's herbal drug.

Down on the beach I plucked up the courage to attempt the water slide. It was at the end of the jetty and stood about fifty metres high. There was also a bar on the jetty serving ice cold beers to assist my courage. I followed the staff member up the steps to the top of the slide. He instructed me to lie flat, cross my legs and place my hands behind my head. What he didn't mention was 'close your mouth'. I screamed all the way down landing in the ocean with a belly full of water.

Back at the hostel I noticed a poster advertising Ladies Night in the bar this evening, promising a room full of men. "Right, Nicci, it's time to make an effort." I thought "Stop sitting in your room, stop being an introvert and go out." I scolded myself.

I got washed, applied some make-up and dressed in a short skirt, floaty top and high heels. I also made a point of removing my mosquito band from round my ankle, which seemed to resemble a criminal tag. And off

I went. On entering the bar, I could see I was not just the only lady in the bar I was also the only customer. Upon enquiring of the Ladies Night, I was told it usually kicked off at about 11pm. It was now 8pm. I sat there for about an hour, on my own, drinking a beer. At 9pm I went back to my room to eat chocolate and watch Netflix.

But I couldn't open my door. It appeared the curtain pole had fallen down and locked me out. I stood on the balcony for an age wondering how I could rectify this. Then American boy appeared. He could see my dilemma and went to get help. He returned with a boy from reception and a boy from the kitchen. Reception boy had in his hand a long metal rod, kitchen boy had a large shiny meat cleaver and American boy proceeded to pull out a dagger from inside his boot. I stood watching as between the three of them they poked, prodded and hacked at my door until miraculously the curtain pole was dislodged. My heroes. My own little Ladies Night.

Chapter 27

The army had arrived! And boy did we know it. Unfortunately, their average age was about twenty-two. Far too young for my interest. They were a lively bunch and were determined to make the most of their two-day R & R. They were full of hilarity and I sat with them until it got raucous, listening to their banter and their plans to 'get laid' that night in town. I politely declined their kind invitation to join them.

"But you're the best-looking Cougar on the island, Nicci." One young army boy pleaded. He had such a beautiful face, toned muscles bulging through his tight t-shirt and a mischievous glint in his eye. "You have to come out on the town with us, I won't try it on. You can trust me."

Somehow, I didn't trust him. Or, was it me I didn't trust?

On their day of departure, they all piled into the beach bar early and ordered beers for breakfast. Their departure time was 2.30pm and they continued to order beers until 2.29pm. Just before they left one of the young boys asked me if I would marry him? Probably the best offer I'd had lately, but, as per, I politely declined.

The second batch of Army boys were due today and apparently they were all officers so would be much nearer to my age. Things were looking up.

I spent the morning lying on a sun-lounger under the palm trees on the beach. There wasn't a cloud in the sky and I amused myself watching the staff set up for today's beach wedding. On the shore line they erected a small altar. They wrapped it in flowing white fabric and adorned it with various fresh flowers. A small selection of chairs were placed on the sand in front of the altar.

The wedding took place just after lunch. I watched the whole ceremony with a sadness inside of me. I was so envious of that bride. Why couldn't it be me? Would it ever be me? I wondered if she appreciated how lucky she was?

Once all the guests had left I wandered over to the altar. I stood under it, looking out across the ocean. I closed my eyes and imagined how it would feel to be a bride. Reality set in when I opened my eyes, looked down and saw my pot belly hanging over my ill-fitting yellow bikini bottoms. As I stood there a good-looking gentleman came over and said, "Now you look like a very lonely bride. Where's your groom?" He introduced himself as one of the Army officers and invited me to join his table for drinks.

Me, the lonely bride...

That evening my Army officer friends invited me to join them on a venture into the town. I politely accepted!

I spent the evening with four officers. Average age about twenty-six! At least they were nearer my age than the first batch. Two were from the British army and two from the Belize army. Unfortunately, all were married or in a serious relationship. But this did not put a damper on my evening. We all had a fun filled night singing, dancing and drinking. Our evening began with beers at the hotel, followed by dinner in the town. There appeared to be some kind of local celebration in the town and the streets were full of people in fancy dress. We did quite a pub crawl and I impressed myself by matching the boys pint for pint. They treated me like an absolute princess and wouldn't let me pay a penny all evening.

Jason, the friendlier of the officers and the most happily married, behaved like a big brother for most of the night. The two officers from the Belize army spoke very little English and spent most of the night locked in their own conversation. Simon, the fourth officer, was a definite lady's man.

"I can't believe your single, Nicci" Simon stated.

"I currently have two girlfriends on the go, back in England. But I could certainly fit you in as my third!" He brazenly told me.

The prospect of being third choice didn't impress me much.

Late in the night I was safely escorted back to my room cradling a banging head and throbbing toes. I passed out immediately and was undisturbed by the air-conditioning that night.

I came down the next morning to find the Army had left, the American boy had left and Mr L was still a distant stranger. I'd been in San Pedro over three weeks now and I didn't belong. It was time to leave.

I'd had plenty of time to reflect on my life of late. I'd arrived in San Pedro feeling damaged, fragile and broken. I'd done a lot of thinking. I'd discovered my limits and boundaries, and my coping mechanisms. My outlook and perception on life, and of the people around me, was as clear as mud. But I told myself that some days were good, some days were bad. So, I would just keep going, one day at a time and just Goddam enjoy and appreciate what is put in front of me. I still wanted my happy ever after, my true love, my husband. But I was also quite sure he wasn't in San Pedro. I would fly back to the UK and reassess my situation. Milo would help me with this.

I had received a few calls from Mr P whilst here. He didn't seem to be coping too well but I knew for a fact me being in his life would not help him. His misguided suggestions that I should return to The Big House were both appealing and frightening. No going back I decided, for his sake and mine.

I'd also received a few messages from Alistair. Quite perplexed that I'd felt the need to run to the other side of the world to get away from him. I assured him he had done nothing wrong and I was extremely grateful for the hospitality he had provided for Milo and me.

I was having one last beer at the beach bar when I spotted Mr L. I cautiously headed over to his table and smiled.

"Hi there." I said. "Just to let you know I'm leaving tomorrow."

"Oh, Hi." he said, "I thought you'd left yesterday."

I'd obviously made no impression on Mr L during my stay. But I chose not take it personally having witnessed how he treated most people around him. He was a big fish in a little pond here in San Pedro. We'd built up a virtual friendship on-line which unfortunately didn't cross over into the real world. Mr L had been extremely kind with his invitation to San Pedro sadly it ended there.

Chapter 28

My journey back to the UK was as exhausting as the journey out. Four flights, four trains, one car and one golf buggy were my transport back. My flight stopovers were slightly shorter and I made sure to wear clothing better suited for each leg of my journey. Sitting on a train in Euston station I closed my eyes and felt confused as the train sped down the tracks. Confused as to why we hadn't taken off yet. Jet lag was setting in.

Looking around the train I amused myself with the possible thoughts of all the other passengers. Was the fat lady wondering what to have for dinner when she got home? Was the young boy, wearing headphones, deciding which tune to download? Was the scary looking thug man hoping to cuddle his kitten later?

Our thoughts are what creates us I decided. They can lay hidden deep inside us, unspoken and private. Or they can be acted upon and define our future. I reflected upon my own. Not so long ago I had thought, to myself, that my life was not progressing in the direction I had hoped for. I had thought 'this is it'. But then I chose to change it. I stopped thinking about it and instead I did it.

I created a plan to find a husband. Possibly not the best of plans but a plan at least. I still believed I could have my happy ever after. But more than that I discovered how wonderful every day of my life already is. I can choose what to have for dinner, listen to a favourite tune and cuddle Milo to my heart's content. I was the same as all the other passengers on this train, but, I thought, I'm making something about it.

So far, on my adventure, I hadn't achieved what I had set out for. But, I wasn't disheartened as it wasn't for a lack of trying. I'd gone out looking,

I'd put myself in situations I wouldn't have previously considered, I'd been to places I'd never heard of and I'd met people outside of my comfort zone. None of this had found me a husband but I'd had a damn good time trying. My blog and social media had opened up so many opportunities for me and introduced me to so many gentlemen. I had no regrets so far. All I had to do now was keep going, keep looking and keep doing.

Back at my mum's house I went bounding through the door shouting out for Milo. Milo came plodding towards me, a slight wag in his tail. Having watched numerous videos of dogs greeting returning soldiers and the like, I was expecting an overwhelming amount of fuss from Milo upon my return. He just looked confused. I felt disheartened. My Milo didn't miss me, it seemed. He sniffed my feet and aimed his gaze towards my hand. Biscuit check, I thought. Then he went back to where my mum was sitting and curled up by her feet. Huh!

Milo and Me...

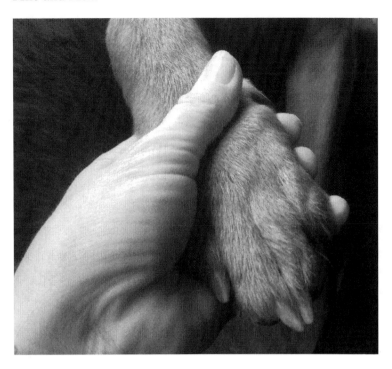

Extracts from my blog miloandme6.blogspot.com

Jet lag and Jaeger bombs - 17th October

I am completely jet lagged. I don't know what day it is or what time. I have taken five flights from Manchester to Heathrow to Detroit to Atlanta to Belize to San Pedro and here I am. I haven't slept for days and now am knocking back beer and jäger bombs at a beach bar in a storm with new friends. How long it will be before I sleep I don't know. I have managed to shower at least. I was so stinky I didn't even want to sit next to myself on the flights!

Thunder storms and traffic violations - 20th October

This weather is crazy. I was so freaked in the thunder storm the other night I was screaming out loud. The building shook with the thunder and the Lightning was right above me. The tin roof did not help my fear. The rain was so torrential I packed a small bag ready for my evacuation! Anyway I lived through it and awoke to a dry muggy day.

I took myself into the town in a golf cart to hunt down a decent coffee shop and found the perfect one on a busy street corner. I was in my element watching the world go by sipping a decent latte. I drove around a bit in the crazy bustling streets and pulled up near the beach. I had a little wander along the storm damaged beach and stopped in a bar for a cold beer and food. I did struggle trying to remember where I had parked the golf cart, there are hundreds of them here and all look the same. I did eventually find mine, it was the one with a 'traffic violation fine' attached to the steering wheel! Mr L kindly took care of it for me.

Last night was to be the bingo night, but everyone got wrapped up in the sport on the TV (baseball I think!) so bingo didn't happen. After too much beer and jäger bombs I hit the sack for an early night.

Today we are having a big lunch hosted by Mr L in honor of his much loved Arsenal football game. We are having roast hams and potatoes and I have been volunteered to make the Yorkshire puds! (I pray they rise to the occasion).

Mr L has informed me that over the next week or so hundreds of army personnel are coming to stay. Now that could be interesting...

Love my air conditioning - 21st October

Today the sun shone bright and hot. I spent most of the day on the beach reading my book. I ate angel pasta pesto chicken and drank light beer. I watched a boy surfing with a parachute, really quite impressive.

Today my air conditioning was repaired after it packed in last night. When I returned to my room it was like being greeted by a huge hug, I am so happy. My neighbour also knocked on my door with a gift of water melon. Life is good...

Missing Milo - 24th October

I spoke to my son today on face time. I've asked him to send me some pictures of Milo. I miss him so much it hurts. I doubt he has even has noticed I've gone, probably thinking I'm taking ages at the shops.

Having so much time to think of late I am wondering how I even ended up here. My life has changed so much and so quickly, half of it hasn't sunk in. In less than six months I've gone from a well-paid job to unemployed. A three bed semi to a motor-home to a country estate to a hostel. From single to fairytale relationship to single. From Merseyside to Scotland to San Pedro. What next I wonder...

Even the army can't save me - 27th October

I've now lost count of how many mosquito bites I have. That rather expensive bug repellent I was convinced to buy has had little effect. And my antihistamines are pretty useless. I'm now wearing an ankle band that makes me look like a criminal wearing a tag. Those little buggers are determined to get me! Besides the mosquitoes the wildlife here is quite friendly, I've met a few wandering around!

The army boys have now arrived and they too have been bitten to pieces so even the army can't save me! They arrived last night but sadly their average age is about 22. They are a lovely bunch and are full of banter and it has been so nice to have some local dialect conversation. I felt I was beginning to pick up a strange American accent and using words like 'awesome'.

It's funny how I've met such a diverse amount of people here on a daily basis and yet I feel so alone. Everybody seems to be here either with someone or for a reason, usually scuba diving. I wish I could have brought Milo, every day I feel like I've lost a limb or something.

My biggest fear at the moment is what am I going back to. I can't stay here forever. I feel homesick but I don't actually have a home. I would really like to keep travelling in my motor-home with Milo as I do still believe my happy ending is out there somewhere...

The next morning, I headed off to the local woods with Milo, who seemed a bit more excited to be in my company now. We walked for about an hour and then took up residence on a bench under the big tree. Milo sat at my feet looking up at me. I looked down at him and said:

"Milo, I need you to pay attention to what I'm going to tell you."

He tilted his big, red, square head with each word I said, never taking his eyes off mine. Except for the occasional sly glance at my hands, always check the hands, if they're closed chances are she could be holding a biscuit.

"We're going away. Me and you, we're going on an adventure, in The Beast, to travel the coast of Ireland..."

THE END, for now

To find out what happens next, read book two to be published later this year. After living in her motor-home in her mum's back garden, Nicci saves up enough money to travel again. Read about her adventures with Milo in Ireland, enlisting the help of a famous matchmaker, going on dates and again attracting media attention. Leaving Ireland and flying off to Portugal with Milo, will Nicci find love in the arms of Mr Hunky...

Please feel free to contact either myself or Milo at;

niccitaylor1@gmail.com

Thank you for reading my book. We would love to receive your feedback;
https://kdp.amazon.com/en_US

https://www.goodreads.com/

Good or bad I can take it, although Milo is slightly sensitive to criticism.

You can read our full blog and keep up with the latest antics of Milo and Me here;

http://miloandme6.blogspot.co.uk/

You can follow us on Twitter at;

https://twitter.com/nicci66nicci

You can see all of Pip's wonderful drawings at;

https://www.facebook.com/PipsPics/

The Prostate Cancer charity who would welcome your donation can be found at;

https://prostatecanceruk.org/ Feel free to mention my name or Milo's when you donate. Many thanks.

Shout-outs; book one

You all helped create my adventure;

Gumtree – for the Beast

Wirral Small Cars – for the TLC you gave the Beast

RAC - for keeping the Beast on the road

The Caravan and Motorhome Club - for many a good night's sleep

Scottish Tourism - for providing some stunning locations

Burns Pet Food - for keeping Milo well fed

Prostate Cancer - for helping my Daddy

Motorhome Full Time - for some valuable information

The Sunday Post - for kick starting this story

Facebook - for new friends and old

Twitter - for new friends and old

IanDavid Hairdressing – for taming my lock

And, Radio, TV and Press, too many to mention - for hearing my voice, for telling my story, for showing my face.

Disclaimer; Please accept my apologies for my lack of geographical knowledge. I have little or no sense of direction and on occasion had no idea where we were!

Printed in Poland
by Amazon Fulfillment
Poland Sp. z o.o., Wrocław